My Sister Helped Me Heal

Vol. 4

Visionary: Chavon Anette

Copyright

Copyright © 2022 by Chavon Thomas

ISBN: 979-8-9869842-5-4

Cover Design: iambiancabrown.com

Printed in the USA:

All rights reserved. No part of this book may be reproduced or used in any manner without written permission of the copyright owner except for the use of quotations in a book review.

For more information, address: www.chavonanette.com

Dedication

To every Co-author who has gone on this journey of sharing their stories as an inspiration to others!

Contents

FOREWORD	I
Biana Brown	
PART I	1
CHAPTER 1	
IT WAS WRITTEN IN HEAVEN	3
By Michelle Franklin	
CHAPTER 2	
MY SISTERS FOUGHT FOR ME	7
By Domonique Renee	
CHAPTER 3	
MY SISTER HELPED ME HEAL	11
By Dr. Joy Durham Harlow	
CHAPTER 4	
I CALL YOU DREAMER	17
By Jasmine Denise	
CHAPTER 5	
TRUST GOD IN EVERY CIRCUMSTANCE	21
By Dr. Dawn Lawrence	
CHAPTER 6	
WHAT MEANT TO KILL ME ONLY DEVELOPED ME	25
By Joy Olds	
CHAPTER 7	
THEY CALLED ME BEAUTIFUL	31
By Kim Brooks	
CHAPTER 8	
ALLOWING JOY TO BE MY PORTION DESPITE OBSTACLES	37
By Ronjeanna Harris	
CHAPTER 9	
HEALING FOR YOUR SOUL	41
By Shywanna Nock	
CHAPTER 10	
RIVERS IN THE DESERT	45
By Michelle Jackson-Brown	
CHAPTER 11	
SISTERHOOD IS A SETUP	49
By Brianna Boomer	

CHAPTER 12
SISTERHOOD CHANGED MY LIFE   53
    By Courtney Ferebee
PART II   57
CHAPTER 13
THE POWER OF PACE AND WELLNESS   59
    By Nadia Hill
CHAPTER 14
ABUSED BUT NOT BROKEN   65
    By Devon Croom
CHAPTER 15
INTIMACY HAS A SOUND   69
    By Jessica Shepard
CHAPTER 16
DELIVERED AND SET FREE TO BE ME, GOD DID IT!   73
    By Antoinette Hines
CHAPTER 17
THE SIGNIFICANCE OF A TRUE SISTER   79
    By Lakeisha Lowe Yelverton
CHAPTER 18
ELEVATE YOUR THINKING   83
    By Que Nona Guilford
CHAPTER 19
BROKEN AND SCORNED   87
    By Madelyn Jones
CHAPTER 20
INCUBATOR FOR WHOLENESS   91
    By Sharnice Sherrod
CHAPTER 21
SEVEN HUNDRED MILES NEVER FELT SO CLOSE   95
    By Brittany Daisy
CHAPTER 22
HER LIFE SAVED MINE   99
    By Alexis Ganier
EPILOGUE
AN UNSTOPPABLE FORCE   103

Foreword
Bianca Brown

Whether inflicted physically, mentally, or spiritually, there is truly nothing worse than being ill, except being both ill and lonely. As a matter of fact, I believe that not having a support system through the healing process does more damage than the illness itself. I grew up hearing, "All I need is Jesus, and I don't need anyone else." And while I understand the theory, there comes a time in everyone's life when we realize that relationships are not just for fun, but its fellowship is a necessity to a healed life and maybe even a life-saving agent. By watching my fellow Christians and even through the lenses of my own experiences, I have noticed that in our zeal to receive the bread of healing, it is easy to overlook some of the people in our life who participate in the healing process.

We are called to lean on the arm of Jesus for our wholeness and restoration. However, if we live long enough, a time will come when the mats of our troubles become too heavy for us to bear alone. Don't get me wrong. We must not mistake the prayers of our friends to be the thing that will heal us, but we must know that our friends simply come along to help us tare off the roof of God's presence and drop us down to the feet of Jesus when we feel like our hands cannot lift any higher and our legs are too weak to stand.

In the thick of our ailment and despair, real friends play a vital role in reminding us of who God is and what we have to live for, and they push us to continue to believe so that we can allow the healing salve of the Word of God to do its perfect work in our lives. This is why *My Sister Helped me to Heal* is such a powerful anthology. The visionary, Chavon Annette, has captured a healing agent and antidote that our world tends to overlook or discount.

Chavon is a world changer by nature, a leader by appointment, and she has brought together a group of women that she believes fit the mold for the assignment of healing in your life. God has placed his fingerprints on this series and is revealing another portion of His healing blueprint even as you read these words. The only thing that I ask of you is that you do not take this journey through this book lightly. I want you to realize that this is God's invitation to you to come on an excursion in the land of God's miraculous restorative power.

I believe that some of us not only just need supernatural healing, but we also need the healing salve that God has deposited into friendships. For some of you, this book will break down the biases you've previously held about friendships. For some of you, God will heal you of your rejection issues. Lastly, I believe there is a special touch for those of you who feel like you're alone. This is your appointed time for restoration, so don't hesitate! Walk through the pages of this book and be healed in the name of Jesus! Amen!

Bianca Brown, *Brand Consultant and Speaker*

Part I

Part I

Chapter 1

It was written in Heaven
By Michelle Franklin

This project has led me to examine the women who have come into my life. As I sat down to start writing, all I heard in my spirit was, "Daughter, it was already written in Heaven." We live in a world that doesn't believe that women can't be connected without drama. Well, let me tell you this. Your relationships are God-ordained. I've had many bad experiences, but I now know the good outweighs the bad. Outside of the woman in my family, I've been blessed with a spiritual mother, sisters in Christ, and even spiritual daughters. I love my life. The peace I have is unspeakable. My faith has increased every time I've had the opportunity to write about my experiences with the awesome women I've encountered.

Women were created to be nurturers. Therefore, we must embrace nurturing our relationship with each other. God didn't just call one woman, but we live in an hour where He's raising a remnant out of women. That means He's using groups. He's pairing us up to get the job done. The women in my life have proven that we can complete each other and not always be in competition with one another. Many women in the Bible remind me of the power of sisterhood and being a woman. Ruth and Naomi, Elizabeth and Mary are the most popular ones. Their stories are being used to shape how we, as women, can submit and glean from one another. I've been single for 20 years. The story of Ruth and Naomi speaks louder because Naomi taught Ruth how to get the attention of the man she wanted. So I ask myself, who is my Naomi? Who is the person who taught me that I didn't have to always sit and wait to be seen by a man but gave me the wisdom on how to position myself to be available to be seen?

About 8 years ago, I had the pleasure of meeting a young lady named Johnette Gore. At the time, she didn't know how important she would become in my life. God used her to help me get home after He informed me that it was time for me to move. That season was very difficult because I was on disability and didn't know who would rent to me. Nevertheless, she made it happen. Within a few weeks, I was moving into a 3-bathroom house. I was excited! Even then, I didn't understand what God was doing or understand the magnitude of the connection. Unfortunately, there was a shift, and we both ended up reassigned to different ministries. We didn't see each other or speak for about three years.

Somehow God opened another door. I was visiting a church, and it just happened to be the church she was sent to. We exchanged numbers and started doing lunch every month. This was God's plan. I was seeking God for a spouse, and I was getting frustrated because I wasn't meeting anyone in the church. One day, we met for lunch, and she told me how she met her guy online. I was like, "NO! I'm not an online person." She said, "OK, but it has worked for others, and it worked for me." I thought about it and decided to get on. Man, I've been getting on and getting off since then. When I told her that these men weren't lining up to my expectations, she rebuked me and said to me that I was too judgmental. She told me to be patient and to stop sizing them up. Be open and use discernment. Her wisdom helped me meet a few good men that have turned into some great friendships. I haven't found the one for me yet, but I've learned to be more open to making myself available to new ways of meeting people.

Not being open to meeting new people and even having high expectations for any relationship can be seen as a sign that a person needs inner healing. Through our friendship, I learned that I set my expectations high because of fear. I was struggling with the fear of rejection, the fear of abandonment, and the fear of being hurt physically. I established these expectations as a safety net. I would often ask, "God, will this man cheat, hurt, or abandon me without notice?" I didn't realize this until He reconnected me with Johnette and I learned about online dating.

These are the kind of women we need in our lives today. Those who will stir us in the right direction and not try and hinder us. For years, I felt like I had been single because of the church. We were taught that God never wanted us to go outside the church and date. This thinking has kept many women single. The men are free to date outside the church, but as women, it's frowned upon. The same leaders who teach us that our spouses need to be men of God are the same ones who found their unsaved wives in the club or supermarket.

Whether I meet him at church or in the supermarket, I will meet him and be ready. I had to realize that my purpose had already been planned in heaven. God had already written it down in heaven that I was going to meet this woman who would change my life, ultimately, for the better. She healed a part of me by opening me up to the possibility of something new. I appreciate her friendship and wisdom, and I love her for all she has been in my life. I thank God for women who are sent to help you heal through the process of your life. God sent all these beautiful women to be a part of my healing process and victories. This book project was another way to heal, and I thank God for this beautiful vessel that was chosen to spearhead it. It was already written in Heaven that I would be a co-author. I pray my story will bring much healing to many women out there. God bless, and go and be great!

Bio:

Michelle Franklin has had the privilege of being trained by The John Maxwell Team, Dr. John Veal, and Dr. Anthony Tiller of American Christian Chaplaincy.

Michelle Franklin has demonstrated effective organizational and communication skills throughout her 19 years in Ministry and the Marketplace. She has exceptional leadership skills, management skills, and is considered a solution-oriented leader. She's skilled in critical thinking and conflict resolution. She is a team player who encourages and influences leaders to mature and flow in one accord. She prides herself in building strong relational and interpersonal skills within teams and believes in professionalism and ministerial ethics to the highest degree.

Some of her experiences include counseling, coaching, speaking, teaching, and training leadership teams. She's a published author of 10 books and is set to release three more in the coming year!

Chapter 2

My Sisters Fought for Me
By Domonique Renee

I remember lying in bed for three consecutive weeks, sinking deeper and deeper into a major depression. My children would peek in occasionally just to see if today would be the day I would get up from the dark hole I had created for myself. They never questioned why I had locked myself in the room day in and day out or why there were so many Hennesy bottles surrounding my bed. They didn't ask why I had kept my room pitch black to block out the sunlight or even why I had gone days without showering or eating. They knew! They had become so familiar with this Cycle that they had witnessed me spiral down so many times in their lives that they just learned how to survive without me until the storm had passed over.

This particular episode was a much deeper stronghold than any of the other ones I had ever experienced. I had so much guilt weighing on me, seeing that I had believed that I had finally overcome the cycle of abuse. I had finally entered a place in my life where I could finally say, "That is no longer my story." I was wrong. I knew that part of the reason for isolating myself was because I was trying to let both of my black eyes and bruises heal. I was ashamed that people always saw me as

Chapter 2

a "Strong" woman but didn't know I was fighting demons that seemed stronger than me.

I was silently crying out for help but did not want anyone to know how broken I was. I was trapped in a place where my mind would tell me that it wouldn't matter whom I told. The wounds were too deep, and no matter how badly I wanted to be healed, my life would always be full of pain. No matter how desperate I was to heal, it never happened, and it never would, and I believed it.

One day, I received a message from a young lady named Amber, whom I had connected with during the pandemic in a prayer group I had joined on a networking site called Clubhouse. There was a Women's Conference coming up that I had agreed to attend, but with all that was going on, I had become so out of touch with how many days had gone by during this time, let alone the date. I remember her being so excited that the date was approaching, and she had asked if I was still planning to attend. How could I? Even if I had the strength to pull myself together and go, I still couldn't go with black eyes. I hesitated to answer quickly, looking to make the best excuse possible, but I couldn't come up with anything.

So I finally told her I would do my best to get there. Her voice on the other end was so full of excitement and anticipation for something major to happen that it started to awaken something in me. It awakened HOPE. I decided to at least try as I promised. I began to try to get the strength to finally move out of the bed I had laid in and drank and cried myself to sleep for so many days. Try to find the courage to look in the mirror to figure out how to expedite the process of healing my bruises. Most of all, TRY to see if God would finally show up to see about me this time.

I finally found the strength to get up from that place and head down to Indianapolis for the weekend to see if there was ANYTHING that could save me on the other side. Amber was waiting for me in the church's parking lot when I arrived. I turned off the car and began to wipe the tears from my eyes, making sure the makeup I had used to camouflage the final healing stages of my bruises was intact. I looked in the mirror and said, "Lord, I'm desperate. If you don't heal me, I will never make it through the rest of this life… I'm TIRED!"

I finally got out of the car, and My sister walked me into the sanctuary. I instantly felt a presence that was very familiar to me because, in this atmosphere, my heart opened almost immediately. The Lord's presence was in the room. This service was different from any other service I had ever attended. The speaker for that night was Apostle Carmen Barnes, who seemed like she was on a sure assignment, almost as a high-ranking Sergeant in the military. She spoke with such Power and Authority! Alongside her was another speaker, Apostle Rein Johnson, who I had been scoping out of the room, and I could feel the deep intercession she had stirred in her concerning everyone in the room. They had come to Wage War on the enemy, and at the time, I didn't know that ultimately in the spirit, they would be the ones to help me fight for my life!

Apostle Carmen immediately felt my desperation and called me to the front. "You there, can you come up front?" I began to walk to the front, nervous because I needed something real. I didn't need another prayer or a prophetic word telling me that God had a plan for my life. I needed to be healed and set free from the demonic chokehold I had been in my entire life! She continued, "You came for something, and you're desperate. You told the Lord that if you don't do this now, I don't think I will come out of this." Instantly, I began to cry. The Lord heard my cry out to him! As she continued to prophesy and pray for me, the women began to labor with me and fight tooth and nail with every deep-rooted trauma going back to childhood.

I remained on the altar that night even after they were done praying because I told the Lord, "I'm not getting up until you promise me that it's over. The torment of my childhood pain, the sleepless nights, the rejection, the abandonment, the suicidal thoughts, the lack of self-worth, my identity crisis, the abuse, substance abuse, and alcohol addictions, everything!" I was desperate to be free!

Chapter 2

That night, God had strategically assigned this group of women to HELP ME HEAL from layers and layers of deep-rooted bondage. Bringing them from all different cities in the United States to fight for my redemption. When I finally got up from that altar, I felt a tangible peace, and the weight of his glory had exchanged places with the weight of the warfare that had been fighting against me my entire life.

I had been set free, delivered, and healed!

To be continued....

Chapter 3

My Sister Helped Me Heal
By Dr. Joy Durham Harlow

It is a part of the human experience that we will know the feeling of pain. The effects of these experiences can often alter our emotions, and sometimes, the result is an experience of trauma. The womanist therapeutic strength-based perspective informs mental health care professionals about the impact oppressive behaviors have on women of color and the trauma that can result. It also helps professionals understand how the strengths women of color have needed to survive the deeply rooted, socially ingrained ideas of hate to become one of their greatest assets. Bryant-Davis and Gobin (2019) explain how acknowledging and understanding these concepts can help trauma survivors heal. Bryant-Davis and Gobin (2019), "By attending to culture, trauma, systemic barriers, and empowerment, mental health providers can provide care for African American women and girls from a strengths-based womanist therapy framework" (p. 18). By adopting these strategies, women might also assist each other through the process of healing.

My first experience with healing came by way of my biological sisters. They taught me to unconditionally embrace who I am, celebrate my African American heritage, love my dark skin, the family from which I

Chapter 3

come, and the enormously rich heritage they had provided their lineage. My sisters taught me that it was ok to say no, to be exhausted, not to like something, or desire to be a part of anything that did not align with my personal beliefs. Through life's lessons alongside my sisters, I understood that I had the right to choose, which changed every decision I would make as I journeyed into my future. My sisters were always present even when physical distance existed. They lifted me at my worst, celebrated my best, and helped me heal. When I was twenty-two years old, I became very ill. I found myself in hospital beds for months on several occasions for the next three years. During these years, I likely experienced the darkest, most uncertain times of my life, as suddenly, my ability to do the things that I had easily previously done was taken away. My fight with chronic illness is ongoing. I have lost my ability to see, walk, speak, write, and do many other things that we often take for granted.

I realize that throughout my encounters with loss, the passion of my biological sisters was duplicated by my sisters in Christ and a myriad of other women from several communities of my past. Their work to help me heal captivated a spirit of service in me that cultivated a passion for serving others and assisting them in their healing process. During these moments, I understood that sisterhood transcended the bloodline and capsulated the spirit of care and nurturing that women innately harbor. These women became a powerful force of active prayer and spoken words of motivation. Many offered physical acts of generosity by cooking and doing my laundry, and these things propelled healing in me that the doctors could not guarantee. These acts of kindness forced a movement inside of me that resulted in a yearning to replicate what I received with an unwavering acknowledgment of other women's individual circumstances to help them heal. As a result, I have accepted the honor of my calling to speak the truth in love, extending this gift of assisting others as they heal through communication.

My career of choice today directly results from the desire to help others. As a Doctor of Counseling specializing in addiction, I serve people whose experiences may have broken their spirit. My career requires assisting people through some of the most exasperating and painful moments of their lives, helping them process through addiction to a successful life of recovery. A part of this process is teaching them not to focus on feelings from the past that are destructive but to embrace optimism and kindness, creating a pathway to the understanding of self through self-love, ultimately experiencing significant growth. Out of the uncertainty of my own experience, I realized I wanted to be a part of the goodness others have shown me. Once you accept that you are perfectly imperfect just the way you are and that you have been called to this very moment to create a life of impact that will outlive your physical body, you are capable of altruistically giving. I encourage others to live by being intentional, spreading light through their words, and cultivating movement in life by responding to their calling.

The womanist perspective grew out of the ideas of womanism. Lindsay-Dennis (2015) defines womanism as "a social change methodology that stems from everyday experiences of black women and their modes of solving practical problems" (p. 6). When embracing other women's struggles, we are learning to understand each other's differences while maintaining the ability to celebrate the strengths we innately harbor. The goal is to be rich in kindness, embracing the same grace given to us, and in this way, we will assist others in achieving optimally successful experiences with life's journey while helping our sisters heal. During the healing process, there is an unveiling that may reveal feelings of being lost, a lack of trust in our instincts, and other beliefs that prevent us from moving forward. And so, the support that collectively arises when women come together to help other women is an organically masterful process that facilitates the deconstruction of decolonization. In this manner, we equip each generation with the necessary tools to become more effective than the previous based on a collaborative effort of growth.

When attempting to understand healing, there must be an acknowledgment of individual experiences. There must be an understanding that every event in a journey is soluble, sometimes, we will need assistance to achieve the goal, yet no matter what destructive pattern you may have experienced, healing can be a reality. I am honored to have experienced healing through my sisters' acts of kindness, and I am humbled to be on this path with you aligning our spirits and celebrating the woman you are called to be.

I want you to see what I see in you.

References

Bryant-Davis, T., & Gobin, R. L. (2019). Still, we rise Psychotherapy for African American girls and women exiting sex trafficking. Women & Therapy, 42(3-4), 385- 405. https://doi.org/10.1080/02703149.2019.1622902

Lindsay-Dennis, L. (2015). Black feminist-womanist research paradigm: Toward a culturally relevant research model focused on African American girls. *Journal of Black Studies, 46*(5), 506-520. https://doi.org/10.1177/0021934715583664

Bio

Dr. Joy Durham Harlow is a mental health professional currently serving as the Director of the Virginia Beach Methadone Clinic (VBMC) in Virginia Beach, Virginia. She graduated from Regent University, where she obtained her Ph.D. in counseling and psychological studies with a concentration in addiction. Dr. Joy previously served as a business executive in Manhattan, New York, for twelve years working on Park Avenue, successfully maneuvering through the corporate world. She was also a professional dancer studying at the world-renowned Alvin Ailey American Dance Theater. At twenty-two, she was diagnosed with a chronic illness that drastically changed her worldview.

Chapter 4

I Call You Dreamer
By Jasmine Denise

At 14 years old, I sat in a psychologist's office, completing their patients' form. The form asked questions such as, do you see things other people do not see? And do you hear things others do not hear? I sat there answering these questions with my mom trusting me to fill out the form. She was unaware I checked yes to the questions because that's not why we were there in the first place. I was hoping that the doctor I was patiently waiting to see would understand me. Tears still fill my eyes thinking about this day. Back then, my grandmother would call me faithfully to pray during the week. I told my mom I was starting to see terrifying things while awake and in dreams, and she shared it with my grandmother. This was happening for a long while, and I just kept my mouth shut.

As the doctor looked over the form, she said, "Jasmine, describe what you are hearing and seeing." My mother immediately interrupted me, "She's speaking from a spiritual standpoint. It's not what you're thinking." I was confused. I knew she was right, but I wanted this lady to help me. Please know my mother is saved, but our upbringing lacked spiritual giftings teaching. While listening, I soon realized I wouldn't receive the help I was hoping for. I just wanted the dreams and tormenting to stop.

Chapter 4

My church announced they were going to a conference in October 2019. World Changers. I had paid for this conference in 2018, but I was a no-show. I knew I had to show up in 2019. If I could find somewhere to lay my head, I was there! I had the courage to ask someone I connected with at church, Charity. She explained her hotel room was full but would reach out to me if someone else needed a roommate. I believe she heard the desperation in my voice. The next Sunday, during the offering, PJ (that's what we call our Pastor) said, "Ask God to give you a number to sow." He explained how many of us would need to stretch our faith once God revealed the number. Listen! The Lord shared a 3-digit number with the unemployed single mom – ME. Let me be honest; I didn't immediately sow. After service, I sat in my car and said, "OK God, I'm going to sow before I pull off, but I must be sure it's you." Sure enough, his gentle touch of peace filled my car. It was time to sow. With my faith stretched and knots in my stomach, I hit submit on my phone. Minutes – not hours, days, or weeks. Minutes later, Charity called and said, "Sis, I talked with the girls staying in the room. We all agreed that you need to be at the conference. You are welcome to come and stay with us. All the beds are taken, but you can have the couch, and everything is paid for. We're not asking you for any money." This day changed my life. Charity, Ebony, Nadine, and Renee had no idea that I was stretching my faith while they were discussing my name. I sat in the church parking lot and cried and praised God for turning my seed around quickly. Lesson learned: Speak up and trust God's way. Usually, I would have stood still doing nothing after God told me to move because I could not afford the trip.

Once they gave me the news, I decided I would drive to Chicago for the conference. While packing to get on the road, my daughter's grandmother called and voiced concerns about me driving alone and far. In so many words, she said, "Flight paid in full!" Wheeew! God was still making way for me to get where he needed me to be. Let me tell you how fear almost stopped my flight. I was so scared to fly. I responded with, "I don't know. I think I should just drive." Crazy right? Drive twelve hours when I can be there in two? I went back and forth. I prayed. My friend says I pray about everything and sometimes I just need to trust God and move – lol. In this case, he was right. A free flight was common sense.

The second night at the conference, the Apostle said, "If you want God to reveal your gifts to you, come to the altar. This moment will change your life." I decided to go. I returned home, and I had a dream the third morning after the conference. I soon realized why God needed me in Chicago. My dreams started and never stopped. Each night. Dream after dream. What I begged God to stop at 14 years old was back. Tormenting, confusing, uncontrollable dreams. This time, I was in a house (church) with language for what I was experiencing. God didn't want me to fear my gift. He revealed it to me. Why would He want that? So, I went to PJ, and he directed me to Lady Wendy, his wife. She was also a dreamer.

Would you believe I didn't allow my children to sleep over at Nana's because of my fearful dreams? My mom would stay on the phone with me all night for me not to feel alone. If I was alone, the enemy would pick on me. I also knew dreams were God's way of communicating with me, but not like this! I'm grateful Lady Wendy's door was always open. She taught me what to say, how to say it, scriptures, and insight. She gave me direction for a gift I was illiterate to. Who knew this was a foundation for a friendship? She coached me out of a season of fear into a season of freedom. Read that again. I've never looked back. Honestly, I've had nights knowing the enemy was hovering over me, and since I was no longer afraid, I became lazy and did nothing. This was not wise. God is very strategic about who and what he reveals. The enemy should not have the authority to enter our space for any reason. Don't become blinded and comfortable as I did.

Each sister I have mentioned helped Jasmine heal. Where would I be without their sacrifices? My mind is safer, I can help my son who's a dreamer, and my gift is still gifting. It's amazing to know that God still calls me Dreamer through it all. The enemy tried to steal my birthright, BUT GOD! Lesson learned: Move and don't stop moving. Dream, and don't stop dreaming. Embrace what God has given. Someone on your path will be instructed to hold your hand. There's freedom in fighting.

Bio:

Jasmine is a Woman of God, a proud mother of Nickolas and Miley, a Project Manager, and an entrepreneur. Having a career in Project Management, she enjoyed the process of turning Vision into reality. This led her to start The Project Bar, LLC. To date, The Project Bar has worked with City officials, nonprofits, and special events to secure celebrity artists like Jekalyn Carr.

A native of Chesapeake, Virginia, Jasmine attended Indian River HS and NSU. She is in the Admin Ministry at church and participates in a Women's Bible Study.

Jasmine has overcome obstacles, including depression and anxiety. Although she sought professional help, the prayers, support, and testimonies of her sisters ultimately helped her heal. Today, Jasmine is an Intercessory prayer warrior intentional about breaking generational curses.

As she soars toward her dreams and aspirations, her saying "In Jesus' Name!" brings hope and happiness to those around her.

Chapter 5

Trust God in Every Circumstance
By Dr. Dawn Lawrence

I grew up in a very loving family, and the love was so fulfilling that I longed to have the same culture as my parents had in my home one day. This infectious environment was filled with laughter, fellowship, and most of all… Jesus. We recognized that our relationship with Him impacted all the other components of our lives. This and other foundational truths were meaningful as a child, but their greatest impact was fully realized when I became an adult and, more specifically, a parent. I was blessed with an amazing father, mother, brother, and two wonderful sisters. We did everything together and learned the power of strong relationships, collaboration, unity, and healthy support. Monopoly, Checkers, Chess, jacks, and Operation were some of the games we often played, especially on rainy days. We ate at authentic Chinese restaurants with tablecloths and took family vacations to Montreal, Canada, and Florida's Disney Land. We attended church regularly and sang as we cleaned the kitchen. So much was done to build a loving culture filled with promise and hope.

As we grew and matured, we went off to college in Boston and Rhode Island and treasured the crisp air of New England. Our bond continued to grow as we learned more about our professional pursuits and the many suitors who expressed interest in dating us. There were many laughs,

Chapter 5

break-ups, and critiques of various individuals. After college, we began to get married and have children. My sisters married and had children before me, so I was the consummate Aunt to my nephews. These bright little bundles of joy were so alert and attentive that it amazed us to see all the new maneuvers they could accomplish each day. We prayed that each would fulfill their Kingdom assignment and have great professional goals. To see my sisters as parents were so special because they were patient, loving, and tender as they nursed each child. Again, this encouraged me to do the same when it was my turn to parent.

My opportunity finally came, and I was blessed to marry my childhood sweetheart. Both of our families rejoiced when we made this announcement because this celebration had been anticipated for many years. Our parents were good friends long before we were born, and all of our siblings and friends attended and supported us in this long-awaited union. After the wedding, we moved away to California, where we began our journey as Mr. and Mrs. Lawrence. We loved being married and postponed having children so we could travel, shop, visit friends, and enjoy one another. Then we decided to start planning for our family. Our first son was born, and my husband had a new buddy… our baby boy. He liked me because I was the meal ticket, but his favorite was Daddy! He was a jolly little fellow who loved to eat and dance. Weighing in at 8 lbs. 12 oz, I had to have a Caesarean, and this was beyond devasting. We took Lamaze classes, ate right, and planned for an amazing, painless delivery… not a C-Section. This was the first blow to my plans for my family. My mother and sisters were concerned about me because they knew how long I had planned for this delivery. Their prayers, presence, and loving support blessed me as my stitches healed and I began to feel better. Since my son was born in November, my family brought Thanksgiving to me in Mount Kisco, New York. My body hurt so much from this shocking experience that I could barely move. Mom was there taking care of the baby and me.

Not long after our first son was born, we welcomed son number two, and I vowed I was finished with that scene. He weighed 10 lbs. and was the complete opposite of his brother. He was robust, strong, feisty, and determined to do things his way. At 10 pounds, he was sure he could make me do what he wanted by yelling and pulling on me. Who was this little tiger?

As they grew and matured, we began to see traits and characteristics which concerned us.

There were specific mild stones that should have been attained and were not. So, the primary care physicians recommended we see the neurologists and developmental specialists as soon as possible. We took them in to see Dr. Montgomery, one of the best in his field. He did a battery of assessments and watched them for three years. He later diagnosed them as being on the spectrum of Autism. This was the second blow to our plans for having a great family.

Being an educator, I knew the implications of such a diagnosis, and again, my sisters and mother were right there with us as we processed this challenge. They provided ongoing presence, prayer, and loving healthy support while loving my sons like their own, spending time getting to know them and instructing them. Their willingness to be selfless and concern themselves with our plight helped us to manage, mature, and maintain our mental stability raising two special needs sons.

Today we are co-authors of *Raising Them "Special,"* a detailed narrative on Amazon, which embraces best practices and strategies that assist parents and caregivers in working with individuals with Special Needs. The book addresses topics such as Parent Advocacy & Support and Establishing Rituals and Routines. We have had the opportunity to share and encourage other families facing similar circumstances. Most importantly, parents and caregivers must take care of themselves before caring for others with rest, vacations, diet, and exercise.

My sisters and I still collaborate, meet, and minister weekly and our message remains the same… fall in love with Jesus and embrace the Word of God for life, freedom, and deliverance found within its pages. For more information, go to prayerschoolglobal@gmail.com or join us on the Prayer School Global zoom.

Bio

For over three decades, Dr. Lawrence has passionately served in the discipline of education. Her career began as a Teacher, Administrator, Consultant, and Senior Coordinator for Compensatory Education. She has a Postgraduate Professional License from the Commonwealth of Virginia in Pre-K-12th grade Administration. As a strong advocate for students and parents, she currently works with the Mind Brain Academy, an entity that seeks to help individuals recognize the "Superpower" found in the brain. Through neuroplasticity, individuals can rebuild neurons, strengthen dendrites, and become better problem solvers.

Dr. Lawrence attended Boston University and Norfolk State University and obtained her Bachelor of Science degree in Elementary Education, master's degree in Urban Education, and a Doctorate in Educational Leadership from Nova Southeastern University in Fort Lauderdale, Florida. Dr. Lawrence presently serves as an Educational Consultant, Author, and Parent Advocate for private and public-school students and parents.

Chapter 6

What meant to kill me only developed me

By Joy Olds

God has an amazing way of carrying us through a learning process. I discovered that these are processes that mature and benefit us. The process has the potential to help grow, anchor, and establish us. From the age of ten until now, I have realized the weight and impact that "process" truly has. Around the age of ten, I received prophecy after prophecy about whom I would become in my future. The prophecies that were told involved me singing and being before many people. As a child, I would see tears fall from people's faces as these prophecies would come. However, I didn't understand what they were so emotional about. I didn't understand the true weight of my voice and the impact it would make until I grew older. I discovered that while God has given me gifts and mantles, the process of maintaining and maturing in them doesn't always feel good. I want to bring you through my testimony of the process and how my aunt, Elder Tara McGee, helped me heal.

In my family, dreams were taught to be valued. Therefore, I value the dreams I have. A specific dream that haunted me as a child and teen was being unable to move or talk. In this dream, my mouth seemed like it had tape within and outside of it. The dreams intensified as I matured and began to understand my gift and mantles. I would sing and get attacked in my sleep. The same would happen after I would minister. Due to the pattern of dreams, I had finally realized that all along, there was an attack on my voice and my identity. However, the attack went beyond my dreams and trickled into my reality.

In my reality, purpose called my name while purpose killers and dream killers were screaming out my name to be bound. Purpose called my name through God's word. My relationship with God became personal and meaningful. He showed me what love and transformation truly were through God's word. As I submitted to God, He began to show me visions about my future and a young women's ministry I would birth called, *Taking Back Our Daughters*. When it came to the season and time to produce Taking Back Our Daughters, that is when my purpose killers and dream killers presented themselves in my life. The dream *killers* were *doubt, fear, worry, incapability,* and *low confidence* in myself. Though they felt like they were *killers*, they helped my development in my process.

I encountered nonbelief about whether I could do what God called me to. I suppressed my true self because I didn't feel it was good enough or could be accepted. In addition, when I should have embraced my differences, I became almost ashamed of them because it was bigger than me. I could see how others treated me and how some weren't too fond of me. It was God's light, anointing, and favor. I began to hold back from saying and doing certain things because of the attention I gave my dream killers. This was a layer I needed to uncover and address, but I didn't have all the necessary tools to do so. I began to talk myself out of what God was telling me to do. However, God gave me another dream, and that was a dream that I was pregnant.

The dream that I was pregnant came after the night the Lord told me to launch Taking Back Our Daughters. I dreamed that my belly was at full capacity, and I had to be careful with the baby. From then, I was reminded of what God showed me I would do. This also assured me that my relationship with God was enough to carry me and help me obey him. With much prayer and positive self-talk, I blindly, with faith, birthed Taking Back Our Daughters in 2018. Over 200 women from Hampton Roads gathered for a one-night gathering. Lives were changed, and people were delivered. However, I could still feel that place inside me, still struggling through the voices of my purpose killers and dream killers.

In 2019, the Lord functioned to host another gathering for young women to unite again within the Hampton Roads area. This year was a trying year. Nonetheless, because of my relationship with God and faith in Him, I proceeded. The evening of the event, nervous thoughts and my purpose and dream killers attempted to take over my mind. A life-changing call interrupted them all and silenced them. It was a call from my aunt, Elder Tara McGee, on an assignment to encourage me. She began to speak into my life about what God was saying about my purpose and the gathering. One of the things she stated was, "Do not fear." Another thing she stated was, "God is with you." She said more, began speaking in tongues, and confirmed my feelings. I was full of tears, and had no true words, but "Thank you so much." Following that moment, I arrived at the Taking Back Our Daughters Gathering, and she was there. She was smiling. From that night, our relationship began.

Unbeknownst, I did not know that God would lead me to join the same church she attended. It warmed my heart that my aunt, Elder Tara McGee, also attended the church. She stood beside me the day at the altar when my father released me to attend church. She protected me, but also my gift. On a particular Sunday, I was heavily wrestling everything that had been layered through suppression. She came to me and helped me - through prayer - break through the layers I knew existed and some I didn't know of.

Next, she told me that I could "no longer water down" myself to be accepted by my peers. All in all, my identity was the main thing I had no

Chapter 6

true sense of because I was suppressing who I truly was for so long. She helped me realize that I had not been treading as God had called me to and that, instead, I was tiptoeing. At the end of the moment, I was very convicted, but I knew it was the best thing that could have happened. I now perceive myself differently. Because of my aunt, I have launched back out into the deep. Lastly, I have discovered the inner warrior in me that I didn't know I had. I am truly thankful for my aunt, who helped me heal and understand the power of my voice and who I am.

Bio

Joy Olds is a native of Virginia Beach, VA, and is the daughter of Superintendent Anthony Olds and Lady Tina Olds. Joy is also a 2018 graduate of Virginia Wesleyan University, where she majored in English. In May 2019, she also graduated from Virginia Wesleyan University with a Master of Arts in Education. She is currently a middle school teacher in the Virginia Beach City Public Schools.

Joy is the founder of *Taking Back Our Daughters,* where her goal is to help lead young women to Christ, educate and help them live their lives and on purpose. She serves on the Church of God in Christ's Young Women in Ministry team, International Youth Department, and the East Region's Young Women in Ministry team. She is also involved in her community. Every Wednesday on Facebook, you can tune in to her empowerment video ministry called "Midweek Joy." Her prayer is that people will see and understand Jesus through her life. Joy is a true testimony that if you are faithful to God, He will be faithful to you!

Chapter 7

They Called Me Beautiful
By Kim Brooks

Sticks and stones may break my bones, but names can never hurt me. This was the rhyme we used to say when someone called you a name. Little did I know that it was a lie. Being called out by your name can crush you. When you are a kid, it can shape the type of person you grow up to be. It can destroy your self-confidence and self-esteem. I never thought in a million years that name-calling was so hurtful.

Friends tend to call each other names jokingly, but is that person joking? Like the first time my friends Lori and Kay called me E.T., I laughed. I thought they were just joking. You know, like we do. But after the second time, their little brother joined in, saying E.T., E.T. I was so mad that I wanted to cry. I felt the tears swelling up in my eyes, so I turned around and walked home with my head down, asking myself what I did to make them start making fun of me. Am I ugly? Why don't they want to be my friend anymore? What did I do? As days passed, I hoped my mom didn't want me to go to the store because I would have to walk past their house. I didn't want to be called E.T. anymore. I was thinking of different ways to walk down the street to the store or to my cousins to hang out. My biggest fear was being called E.T. one day at

Chapter 7

school, walking through the halls. What an embarrassment that would be. They are supposed to be my friends. We hung out all summer. I didn't understand. Why? Why me?

This was worse than always being called ugly or a baby by family members. I couldn't tell anyone about what I was going through. Fearful they may start calling me E.T. as well. I was alone, holding in this horrible secret, wallowing in my pain but smiling like nothing was wrong. My self-esteem was being kicked, punched, chewed up, and spit out. On top of getting called E.T., there was you're ugly, you talk like a baby, and you can't sing. My sister was the main person that tortured me by telling me I was ugly or I couldn't sing.

I knew I wasn't a singer, but I loved to sing with Whitney Houston. I had her first album, which I played all the time. I always tried to wait until my sister would leave the house before I would start singing. I found enjoyment and peace when singing. Going through these things did something to me. It made me start looking closely at whom I called my friend. I started pulling away from making friends with other girls. My trust in them wavered. I became closer to my male cousins and their male cousins playing 2 square and 4 square, going swimming, climbing the Blackberry tree, and a lot of other fun things. They didn't call me names or make fun of me, which felt good. I trusted them! I felt safe with them!

As the years went by, I became a loner. I didn't seek friendship with females. I went to work, took care of my daughter, and went to sleep. Then do it all over again, day after day, month after month. Until I started to feel truly alone, and depression started to set in. So, I decided to try letting females into my space. I decided to put them in categories to control the possibility of being hurt again. My categories were associates, friends (no more than 3), and clubbing. The associates were the girls I was cool with and spoke to, but they couldn't get too close because of the vibe I got when talking to them. Then the ones that had the pleasure of being my friends would go shopping, out to eat, and go to the movies.

We would visit each other's homes. They knew my kids. I knew their family. We could talk about secrets freely and not have the fear of being ridiculed. Now my clubbing friends were exactly that. We would club on Fridays and Saturdays, drinking, dancing, and just chilling in our section of the club. When the club closed, we went our separate ways and may not speak to each other again until mid-week to make plans for the weekend. Finally, I was in control.

So, as I began to get older, and after some tragedies in my life and no more clubbing, I felt like I was missing something in my life. I didn't know what it was. I tried clubbing again by myself, but that didn't feel the same. I started to feel lonely, unfulfilled, and unsafe while trying to fight the depression. Then one day, my oldest daughter invited me to church. My first thought was I'd already tried this once before, but I went. I told myself I would go with her, but I didn't want to talk to anyone. We ain't making no new friends! The thoughts of my past church home in Ohio came rushing back. I had one friend I used to go shopping together and go bar hopping on the weekends. She knew my kids and we worked at the same job. Just one day, she stopped talking to me. She would see me at work and turn her head, going the opposite way if she saw me at the store. I never found out why she stopped talking to me. I concluded that it was jealousy. However, I still went to church with my daughter with those thoughts in my head. I didn't want to let her down. Then I went back the next Sunday and the next Sunday. Before I knew it, I found out what was missing in my life. That feeling of being lonely, unfulfilled, and unsafe started to fade away the more I attended church. I was still interested in making friends, but there were some ladies that I said, Hi to or waved at.

After a couple of years of being back in the church, it became a routine more than fulfillment. One Sunday, it was announced that the Youth Pastor would be leaving and starting his church. I knew the Youth Pastor from a previous job, and I enjoyed it when he preached on the 4th Sunday. Well, I decided to follow him. I became active in the church in

Chapter 7

the Children's Ministry, where I served with ladies I didn't know. My first instinct was to be quiet and not interact with them, but these ladies made me feel comfortable. There was something different about them.

Now let's jump ahead about three years. Once again, I had that feeling that something was missing in my life. I was hearing other ladies in the church talk about projects they were doing, and it sounded awesome. One of the ladies was a Life Coach, and her name is Chavon Thomas. I decided to inquire about what she offered, thinking that was what I needed. I began to have meetings with her as my Life Coach. This was uncomfortable because I had to talk to her about some personal things, and I didn't know her from a hole in the wall. Our connection progressed into a mentorship, which opened me up even more, and connected me with different kinds of women. It was weird to me because I was more comfortable with women as Chavon and I grew in entrepreneurship. *These women are different,* I thought once again. Chavon founded Power and Grace Leaders, a movement to strengthen women to fulfill their potential and purpose on this earth. Being a part of this movement is one of my greatest decisions. The ladies don't judge who you are, what you've done in the past, or what you may be struggling with. Chavon Thomas and the ladies of the Power and Grace Executive Team have introduced me to my present self, and I love it.

Bio:

I was born and raised in Mansfield, OH. I moved to Richmond, VA, in 1998 with my two daughters, Kayla (8) and Lachelle (11). We have lived in 4 of 7 cities here in Hampton Roads. In 2013m my oldest daughter made a grandmother to my handsome and creative grandson Elijah. I am the CEO of Transition Credit Counseling, a Certified Financial Business Coach, a Credit Repair Counselor, and a Certified Fire Leadership Coach. A member of the Power and Grace Leaders Executive Team. I am a big fan of DC Comics and Marvel movies. I'm a die-hard San Francisco 49er Fan and a University of Michigan Football Fan. That's right, I'm from Ohio, but I Love Michigan… Go BLUE!!!

Chapter 8

Allowing Joy to Be My Portion Despite Obstacles

By Ronjeanna Harris

Looking at my journey was very uncertain during my early adulthood. I carried so many unhealthy weights of defeat from not properly facing battles. This created hard cycles of lessons for me. I often would doubt my worth. The funny thing is I would bottle up the emotion of feeling like a failure at everything, often making me think that the bare minimum was ok. Don't get me wrong, I would have fun and hang out, but there was a huge void because I felt I didn't deserve joy because of all my mistakes so far. I would overcome and then go right back into thoughts of feeling undeserving. Later in adulthood, I found out that these were strongholds. I didn't want to embrace the grasping of true worth and my chosen hood. I started getting punctured emotionally with the stings of life and did not get the triage necessary to come out of enclosed moments of hurt. I was scared to let folks in. I didn't want to fully uncover and unfold for results of breakthroughs during these moments of my life journey. I was so familiar that for a long time, I made myself believe that I was perfectly fine and that it would get better with

Chapter 8

no one's help or assistance. See how the build-up can make us blind from the true reality. I had more justifications than a man going to jail, lol.

This build-up cost me to start letting go of what was important while still functioning like every day; many didn't know it. I would have multiple attacks of panic because I kept so much in. As a child, I could see (Seer) but didn't understand my gift, so I felt like no one could see that I was dying on the inside. (Whew) This was my thought at that moment, and I was progressing my goodness too fast. I had two little girls, a single mom at the time. Trying to figure out life and the many why's, I often pondered. When provoked, I had a temper that would spiral out of control because of improper healing; it would bring on behaviors that were not of good judgment. God kept me during those times because it was his grace and mercy that I didn't end up in jail somewhere. I'm yet managing to succumb to the days broken. Deep down inside, there was a yearning and fight to have joy like the bible teaches us. That meant there was a press that could lead to healing with God and guidance from great women. There were women assigned to me; I just haven't met them yet. I knew that my girls deserved the best of me and not just any version of me. First of all, they were just a loan to me from God, and it's indeed a privilege to experience motherhood, no matter the circumstance.

I have learned that there are levels and stages of healing in one's life. It is a different experience for everyone because life and journey have been on so many different routes. I came to the Hampton Roads area in 2001 with my now husband. (We were dating at the time) I attended a local church and eventually joined, and the ladies there showed so much confidence in their worth. It was amazing. I wanted to feel excited about myself and have joy that bubbles from the inside. Those Kingdom Queens ignited me to want to be healed from that season of having low self-worth. The next set of queens that provoked and ignited me to journey to obtain this healthy proceeding to get my inner joy was my two daughters, Kestasia Smith and JyAsia Smith. Wow, my daughters were the sisters that helped me heal during this season I encountered. They

Allowing Joy to Be My Portion Despite Obstacles

deserved the opportunity not to have their joy tainted. I had to make sure I dismantled the generational transfer. This was another eye-opener for me. I had to want it for myself before I could healthily show someone the way. That made me want to make sure I did my part to let people understand that we were created to have unspeakable joy dwelling on the inside. I was able to heal properly from spiritual reflux, my God from zion. You can do the same if you feel like your joy is gone or you never really experienced it in its fullness. That stops today. The Bible tells us in several scriptures that joy is our portion. I thank God that I survived that season. God was keeping me even in my battles. And to know that my two daughters help me so I could be the best mother for them.

I want to encourage the reader to hold on to that inner fight to be whole, joyful, at peace, healed, and free from the inside. Never be afraid to grow, learn and talk to a trusted source. Jesus and therapy are a dynamic collab that gets through the layers and build-up of trauma, hurt, rejection, and pain from life. Your purpose deserves the best of you to complete the goals and mission you are on to be great and help others. People are waiting on the very testimony you will have because of healthy overcoming. Always seek God, and never doubt him. Jesus will never fail you. Strong prayer life is as important as reading the bible. We must be fed good spiritual nourishment as the bible teaches us. Remember, you are uniquely and wonderfully made. (Bible) Speak life, declare joy every day you open your eyes. Dismiss and dismantle negative thoughts. Love yourself unconditionally. There is a sister assigned to your life to help you heal and vice versa. Be well mentally, physically, and spiritually. I pray this read encouraged you to continue your purpose in excellence. You deserve to win. You deserve to have great joy.

Bio

Ronjeanna Harris is a God-fearing and chosen ordained Evangelist, affirmed Prophet, and Intercessor. Ronjeanna is a devoted wife, mother of six, and grandmother of two. She is an LPN with over twenty years skill and experience in healthcare. This game-changer is the proud owner of Just Jeanna's Skin Care LLC. Natural Product creator & Formulator was launched as a company in 2018 after much prayer, research, and preparation. After two years in business, Just Jeanna's Skin Care LLC got approved to be in the Walmart marketplace in 2020. Ronjeanna is a five times Amazon #1 best seller Author, LPN, and award-winning Certified Wellness Coach with over 20 years of experience and skill in the healthcare industry. Just Jeanna's Skin Care LLC offers a host of local, national, and international services. This trailblazer, in May 2021, started her nonprofit organization, Jeanna's feed, doing what she loves, which is being a servant. Jeanna's IFeed has a multi-award-winning nonprofit known for its esteemed consistency of serving the communities in the Hampton Roads and Eastern Shore of VA. Kingdom Solutionist coaching & mentoring services was birthed in 2021. Community serving and giving back is an honor and passion for Ronjeanna. She is a proud member of Cornerstone City Refuge Global Alliance (The New City Church of Va) under the Leadership of Apostle Dannie and Pastor Rebecca Ducksworth, serving as Evangelist. Providing natural wellness solutions is Ronjeanna's mission to stand by.

Chapter 9

Healing for Your Soul
By Shywanna Nock

I could share a lot about the things that I have been through. I know that many of us share similar situations. I know that all of us decided to put those difficult situations in God's hands. I can recall during 2011, I experienced excruciating pain in my arm for several months. I went back and forth to the doctor to find out what was going on with me. The doctors told me that it was probably a pulled muscle. I was always told to listen to my body. I was at work, and the pain was too much to bear, and my breathing was off a little bit. I made up my mind to get checked out fully. I went to my doctor and told her the issue that I was having and demanded to get a chest X-ray. I am glad I chose to get the X-ray because I wouldn't have known what was going on with my body. The doctor discovered that I had a mass in my lungs. I went through all the procedures of testing the mass to ensure it wasn't cancerous. The next plan was to remove the mass, but that didn't happen. A simple procedure of going in and removing a mass turned into a diagnosis of cancer. I was diagnosed with Non-Hodgkins Lymphoma at the age of 34. I can remember that day as if it was yesterday. My life was turned upside down. I was a single mother and just received bad health news.

Chapter 9

I was numb and didn't know how to process the news I was hearing. I knew at that moment I didn't have control of the situation. The human side of me wanted to cry and give up, but I knew my kids depended on me. I didn't have an opportunity to process what was happening. I was told that I needed to start chemo right away. I went from surgery to chemo in three days. I knew that I needed God to help me because this was a situation that I couldn't handle. Once I took the chemo, my body instantly started rejecting the treatment. I felt something was wrong and started to get discouraged. I wanted to give up because it wasn't what I expected. My mother and father were there, and she grabbed my hand and began praying. I immediately calmed down and started to relax. She started to encourage me, and then my nurse began talking to me. My nurse reminded me that this sometimes happens when you're being administered chemo for the first time. She reminded me that she would do all she could to help me get through this. She told me I needed some other medicines before starting again. I prayed to God to calm my fears during this process. The medicine was administered again, and it flowed like it was intended to. I stayed in the hospital for two weeks. During my time there, I would always watch the inspirational channel. I saw a service where a woman was diagnosed with cancer. She went to the church and had the saints to pray that God would heal her. She returned to the doctor and was told that the cancer was gone. I praised God and shouted for her because I knew He would do it for me too.

The test that I was going through was a challenging one. I had faith in God, but this caused my faith to go to another level. I praised God in the midst of all that I was going through. I praised him while I had strength because I knew the chemo would have me down for a few days. I was drawing strength when I needed it. My family, friends, and church family were very supportive during my time of need. And I learned to speak the word over my situation. I looked up healing scriptures, and I constantly spoke them throughout my life, even though my circumstance was different at that moment. A lot of people in my life encouraged me daily not to give up. I would go into the house of the Lord and give God the praise for just being alive. My mother always pushed me to dance for God, even when things were bad. I danced and praised God until times got better. I knew my healing was on the way and pushed through the storm until God said, it's done.

I can truly say that I've been blessed. I have a testimony that I will continue to share with the world, and tell of his goodness and how he brought me out. My testimony is going to change lives. I am a true example of what God can do. You can make it with God on your side. You have to pray and seek him even when it looks bad. You have to keep your eyes fixed on him regardless of what you're going through. You have to change your way of thinking and focus on the positive outcome of your situation. God didn't bring any of us this far to leave us. You can see that God did it for me. I am an 11-year cancer survivor. I didn't quit in the middle of the battle. God met me there, and he proved to me what he could do. I just needed to trust him. God isn't finished with me. I have so many people that need to be reached. God is saying, "Don't stop and don't quit. I will give you the strength to overcome what you're going through." I allowed him to work it out, and I am standing here today to testify that he made a way.

Bio

Shywanna Nock is a mother of three. A motivational speaker, the author of Cancer had my body, but it didn't have my mind, Amazon Best Selling Co-Author of Joy Comes in the Morning, Founder of Nay-Nay's Inspirations, CEO of Marketing, Financial, Certified Life Coach, and Creative Services of Onpointradio Station. She loves giving encouraging words to uplift someone's day. You can connect with her at: www.shywannanock.com, empoweryourself76@gmail.com.

Chapter 10

Rivers in the Desert

By Michelle Jackson-Brown

Upon the insistence of my biological sister, I finally found my church home. It was a few years into my journey with Jesus and two churches later. I had sustained wounds from a previous church, and this place allowed me the opportunity to heal. I remember walking into this church and hearing the Lord say, "Freely you receive, freely you give." There was no demand placed on me or my giftings. I was able to sit for a couple of years and worship and be washed by the word. One day in my private time with God, I heard him say, "You've sat long enough - ENGAGE!" I wasn't talking to anyone at the church nor attending any extracurricular events. It was around the fall of 2013, and my church was hosting classes. A woman of God, now one of my closest friends, was teaching a class called "Help, My Faith Won't Work!" This class helped me identify some things that were in my heart that were holding up my breakthrough. It helped me heal along the way. I remember her saying, "God is telling you that it is time to do what he has told you to do!" I knew she was talking to me. Shortly after, the next month, I relaunched the ministry God gave me years prior. God's favor was all over it.

Chapter 10

Next, I heard the Lord say, "SERVE." The following Sunday, I was in the video cafe service at my church, and they needed volunteers. I filled out a form, and two days later, I received a phone call from another sister who would also help me heal and grow in my journey with Jesus. I remember this day just like it was yesterday. She called and wanted to set up a time to meet. I told her that I was available to meet that day, and we ended up meeting at the church. While describing the available volunteer positions, she stopped and said, "Holy Spirit is telling me that there's something that you need to talk about." Honestly, I was a bit hesitant and didn't want to open up, but God showed me that she was a safe place. I began to share with her that a sister was tired. I owned and operated a full-time independent insurance agency alone. I was a mother of two student-athletes, a wife, and a sister to many. My relationship with God was amazing, and He was growing and developing me rapidly. I was so busy pouring out and being there for others that I was depleted. I had a consistent prayer life, devotion, and established quiet time with God, but something else was missing.

She prayed for me and journeyed with me for a short period, but she made a great impact. Many days while serving in the café, she would say, "Michelle, that's enough. You need to go sit under the word; I can handle it from here. I get paid to do this." Another powerful thing she said to me was, "Michelle, you are a servant at heart, and you have to protect that because some people will take advantage of it and leave you dry!" Isn't that the truth? This sister was a blessing to my life! She was a sounding board and cared for me beyond my role as a volunteer. She took time out with me, and we would mastermind for business. She was a businesswoman and a woman of wisdom and integrity.

I remember one particular Sunday; she invited me to join her after church with her family. We sat at the table and discussed the word the pastor taught that day. There were a couple of business owners there, too, and we shared ideas on ways to improve business. I was ready to give up on my business, but they gave me ideas on how to refresh it. I thought to myself, "Here I am, sitting with a table of strangers who want to help me and see me prosper." Others in my past seemed only to see what they could get from me. It was a breath of fresh air! This sister took out her time and we would meet every Tuesday for business. She introduced me to a book called, "Think and Grow Rich" by Napoleon Hill. We read it together, discussed it, and she ministered to me. We would discuss prophetic dreams and interpretations. She provided a sense of family and community I honestly did not have in the Body of Christ. The church I attended was huge, which was fine for me because I didn't want to engage until I was ready. However, she became the balance I needed on a small scale to engage, heal, and grow at the same time. She was a bridge toward the restoration of my serving in the church. God knew who, when, and how he would do this for me. He used this sister to restore my hope and showed me that not everyone is out for themselves. She never attempted to see what she could gain from me. She allowed God to use her as a healing agent in my life. She showed me what a true faith community looks like and what the church should look like. I am forever grateful to each sister that served as a gatekeeper to my healing process. Thanks to my sisters: LaKeisha, Donnesha, and Rhodonna, who helped me heal.

Bio

MICHELLE Y. JACKSON is a woman of faith who is called to the marketplace. She is an entrepreneur, broker/realtor, and Life Coach with a heart for Jesus. She is also strongly passionate about the treasure in the field, that treasure being God's people and helping them run with purpose. She desires to reach those who are lost, oppressed, broken-hearted, and discouraged.

Michelle is dynamically motivated by God to bring out the best, most successful opportunity for anyone with whom she is associated. With each challenge, Michelle allows God to lead and guide her in developing a battle plan, whether buying or selling a home, writing a devotional, speaking, praying, or leading a group. She desires to see all live the abundant life that Jesus gave us through understanding their purpose and identity in him.

Chapter 11

Sisterhood is a Setup
By Brianna Boomer

Yep, A SETUP!

Let me explain…

I was that cool young girl from around the way. I thrived in knowing I was in the crowd, what I had seen on TV. Find friends and do everything, including losing myself and my values to keep them. They were my girls, and we had a lot of good times, but the question is, "Were they good for me?" Late-night parties, drinking, constant pressure to have sex, drugs, unclear future paths, with a splash of church every six months. I felt like I had water down who I was to fit in. So I would say the clear answer is no, but remember, this is a setup. (To place or erect something into position "webster."

NO NEW FRIENDS the motto kept me bound for years, feeling like I owed them my loyalty because we were bonded through trauma. My day one's, my ride or dies. We had an emotional connection based on our pain, experiencing similar traumas. I feared losing them, and they made me feel validated. But God was calling me higher. I could feel I was called to do more, to be more, that there was a better life somewhere out there for me, AND I WANTED IT. Everything began to change. I focused on

Chapter 11

school (I was the only one who went to college after high school), got a new job and car, and even started going back to church.

I knew of God, but I didn't know him for myself. Struggling with fatherless issues, I didn't clearly understand what a father was or what a father did. While trying to build a relationship with Christ, He cleared the way one by one. I stated losing friends, small arguments turned big, emotions and envy arose, and we were just not clicking anymore. But I felt like I was losing myself in that process, I was hurt and disappointed, and that spirit of abandonment surfaced. They did the same thing my father did, the same thing my mama did when she went to jail. The same thing I felt like God had done. I thought I wouldn't be left again if I did everything to fit in. I knew my limits. So I gave up on friends, kept people at a distance, and let them in enough but not too much. Somehow, I reconnected with Courtney, a cousin on my dad's side (she's in this book too). This relationship started off rocky. I was distant, lying about hanging out with her. Why would I hang with someone who reminded me of my pain, who carried the same blood as the person I wanted the most but who didn't want me (My Father)? She didn't give up, invite after invite. This girl was consistent, so I gave in. She was cool, and I began to see we were very similar good and bad. Almost like twins, this still amazes us to this day.

A few years later, we became tight. When you saw her, you saw me. But with her came constant reminders of my pain. There were family events that I didn't welcome because I was holding so much hurt towards my father. During this time, I had no choice but to start healing. I became aware of how I felt and addressed my emotions. Something I knew I needed to do because it was taking a toll on me. Bitterness and unforgiveness didn't feel good, it didn't look good, and it overflowed into everything I was producing. I was getting better. Having hard conversations. (Some parents couldn't be good or present because they didn't know how to, they were struggling with their battles and unaware of their hurtful actions because they were hurt too, so give them grace.)

One conversation with my father broke so much of me. Letting go of that hurt felt good, but I was still looking for love in all the wrong places. I didn't know what it was, how it looked, or how I was supposed to be loved or treated. I just knew that I wanted it, and that came with a lot of lessons looking for it. I realized I was looking for me the whole time. Brianna, the girl in the mirror, I avoided because she hid so much pain because she wore a thick mask. Still, God knew exactly what I needed, a push, someone who would go through healing with me, the mood swings and isolation associated with finding myself. A person whom I didn't have to question whether she would leave me. My sister would be there for my highs and lows. My sister would ask the hard questions and listen to the broken answer, the one who would help me heal. So here I am today, experiencing healthy friendships with amazing women, including Courtney. FREE from my past hurts, acknowledging my wounds and still healing. I have found me, the me I was when God created me, me beyond the hurt, shame, and issues I have experienced. And that was the setup. God set me up to heal, remove the dust, and find Brianna B. It IS NOT my day one's that are still holding me up. It's my day eights. So be open-hearted when God is changing your circle. He wants more for you. He will use everything you have been through and all of your flaws, strengths, gifts, and challenges to set you to be your best self, who he created you to be. The setup was necessary for me to be in this position today to tell my story of how my sister helped me heal.

Roman 8:28

"And we know all things work together for good to them that love the lord and who are called according to his purpose."
 IT'S ALL WORKING TOGETHER FOR YOU; THE SETUP IS FOR YOUR GOOD.

Bio

Brianna Boomer, also known as Brianna B, is a world changer. She was born and raised in Norfolk, Virginia, where she's currently a Teacher for the Public School System. She has a degree in Human Services, Psychology, and Education and will soon be a Master in Community Counseling. She aspires to empower people to use their strengths to overcome limiting beliefs, develop skills, build confidence, and produce real results in their personal and professional lives. She does this through being an empowerment coach, social media influencer, community advocate, and educator, and most of all, spreading joy, love, and a splash of laughter amongst everyone she encounters. Her life motto is "Life is what you make it." This pushes her to help herself and others Believe Bigger, Achieve More, and WIN on and in Purpose!!!!

Chapter 12

Sisterhood Changed my Life
By Courtney Ferebee

I never knew sisterhood would have so many lows. I've experienced betrayal, rejection, negativity, and so much more. Growing up, I had so many friends. For instance, I need your hands and feet and mine to count how many friends I had. At that moment, I didn't know what sisterhood meant. I thought we were all right as long as we talked, had sleepovers, and went to the mall. I've had my sister damage my car "on accident," talk behind my back, and even got into a relationship with my ex-boyfriend. And that's just to name a few. I was taken advantage of a lot because I would give my sisters the last shirt off my back. Anything they needed, I made sure they had and much more. I knew at some point I was not being treated like I should. I was pouring out so much love to them and receiving little to non-back from me. As time went on, it got very draining to the point I had nothing left to give them.

I love extremely hard. Letting people go was something that I struggled with for a very long time. I am sure you are thinking I should let them go with all that they have done! Nope, there was still something in me that I would still contact to ensure they were okay. I would still make sure they would receive a call from me and a gift on birthdays. I wanted to still let them know that I would always be there for them no matter what. As time went on, my family ended up moving to a different city. I hugged them and never looked back, and I never wanted a sisterhood again because I thought it was full of lows.

Fast forward ten years later, I joined a church called transformation church. I met a couple of friends that became sisters. At this point, I just knew I came across "PERFECT SISTERS." Our names were even unique (ABCDE) Aresia, Brianna, Courtney, Domonique, and Ebony. Brianna is my cousin, but we all became a sisterhood. We started hanging out more, doing bible studies and road trips; we have so many things together. At this point, I still have not healed from past sisterhood hurt. I was expecting the same woman to do the things I was used to. In the beginning, I did not get too close because I knew I would have to let them go at some point!

I asked God, if these were not the sisterhood for me, then remove them because this was too good to be true. The devil must have heard that prayer because our relationship took a turn for the worst. In my mind, I thought I knew this was going to happen to me. God began to deal with me at that moment concerning this sisterhood and how they have helped me to become a better sister and not expect the worst from them because of my past. I began to weep. I called E(Ebony), we went to lunch, and we laid it all out. Shortly after, we became close again. We had a sleepover and cried and cried for hours. We began to tell each other how we have helped each other in different areas of our lives.

I had to pause for a moment because not one time did any of my sisters betray me, make me feel less than others, or have any negativity. We all embraced each other. We have all experienced past hurt when it came to sisterhood. We assured each other that we would always be together to the end, and it didn't matter how far we went. As we began to support and love each other, I began to heal from my past and not expect any disappointments.

Sisterhood Changed my Life

I love my sisters, and there is nothing I would not do for them. I thank God, He put us all together, and it was a divine connection. We have experienced so much together, which made our relationship even closer. I had to remember every day would not be sunlight, but it was worth the fight; every relationship requires work. If it was not for my sisters, I would not be at this place in my life right now. They have pushed me beyond what I thought I was capable of. I've had shoulders to lean on, a shirt to wipe my tears, a listening ear, and more.

After all of this, we are not as close as we were; one sister moved to Georgia to pursue her career. When we all see each other, it feels like nothing have changed. As sisters, sometimes you can grow apart, or life experiences happen, but at the end of it all, we will always be there for each other.

If you do not have a sisterhood, I encourage you to get one. If I did not, I would have made friends on top of being hurt and continue to be hurt because I did not know what sisterhood meant. Since this divine sisterhood, I was able to launch businesses and books and even have a closer relationship with my biological sister. We all need a sisterhood; you cannot do life by yourself! We all need accountability and support from your sister. Makes life easier, and you don't have to experience all your lows or highs by yourself.

Be encouraged, and God will connect you with the right people at the right time. Sisterhoods become lifelong friends that grow old together and become more like family. I started this sisterhood hurt and disappointed, and now I am healed and loving on all my sisters and also preparing for what other connections God will allow for me. If you are reading this, stay strong; this is how my sisters helped me heal.

Bio

Courtney Ferebee is a confidence Coach. She helps women and teenagers redefine their confidence through identity and purpose. She is also the author of a children's book, Lauren Saves The Bully. Courtney has a nonprofit organization for teenagers called Confidence Beauties Mentorship Program. She loves helping and uplifting through motivational speaking and social media influence.

Part II

Chapter 13

The Power of Pace and Wellness
By Nadia Hill

We live in a society where convenience is praised and normalized. This has been an influencing factor toward success, connections, and daily living. I've overcome different experiences without considering the necessity of pacing. It allowed me to learn that every twist and turn produced a level of rigor and grit. Also, my perspectives were challenged to see the healthier alternative to those life experiences. In August 2015, my family and I were evicted from a place we once called home. I'll never forget the hard pounding on the door and directives from the Cook County Sherriff. My younger sister and I rushed downstairs to grab anything we could fit into our backpacks. I felt vulnerable, disappointed, scared, and defeated. This was the beginning of my undergraduate senior year at the University of Illinois at Chicago (UIC).

I was met with overwhelming pressures and anxiety at the tender age of 24. My family and I sat in deathly silence. Exhaustively, my mother began to weep while my brother was consumed with anger and exited the car. However, my younger sister and I knew we couldn't afford to crack

Chapter 13

under this pressure. We began to throw out different relatives we could reach out to. Then, I remembered that my grandmother had some space at her house. This brought some relief because I knew I could focus on my classes and graduate in December 2016.

Sadly, my mom's mental state was declining due to the unexpected passing of my grandfather in May 2015. She was grieving her father's death during a very fragile season in life. The burdens of a single mother were demanding, never-ending, and weighty. Her aspirations and desires were sacrificed for the well-being of her children. Naturally, her resiliency gave her the strength to plow through, but what about her Good Samaritan? My aunt opened her house for my mom and sister to stay in. This was a needed victory to pace during this homelessness journey. Sadly, my brother had to stay with some friends and associates during this intense life experience.

My brother was attempting to distance himself from us. He felt guilty due to his associations with the wrong crowd. He felt the need to purchase a gun for protection. But he didn't think his family would be affected by this impulsive decision. Our former apartment was owned by Chicago Housing Authority (CHA), and certain policies were written to prevent certain illegal activities. Surprisingly, CHA found out that my brother was jailed for possessing a gun. This affected the stability of our livelihood, and we were removed from the lease without hesitation. Sadly, my brother's journey of homelessness was more traumatic due to his stay at an overcrowded shelter.

Understanding how to pace during my life experience created peace. I was accustomed to achieving my desired goals without thinking about the mental stress that comes with them. Surprisingly, I was experiencing a lot of mental and emotional stress due to how I was treated while staying with family and associates. I began to think about ways of managing the stress, which led to cultivating a passion for mentorship. It felt like a lightbulb switched on when I was able to talk to blooming young women about attributes of Godly femininity. Naturally, mentorship created the space to develop the peace needed for my homelessness journey. I noted that being a mentor required a detailed plan for each mentee. And the pacing of their growth identified the importance of pace in my life.

Immediately, I began to create weekly time management schedules to ensure high levels of productivity and support. My homelessness journey showed me that the lack of support ensured blind spots went unattended. Consistently, I was highly productive but overwhelmed by anxiety and worry. I'd mastered the art of deception to interact with those close to me. My obsession with appearing "strong" warped my perspectives about a healthy community. But it forced my hands to never disconnect from finding my pace again. As a result, the tools of pace, rest, and healthy community were cultivated during my journey.

Beautifully, I grew in maturity, pace, and healthy community. I began to take ownership of underdeveloped areas, such as poor spending habits, emotional intelligence, and dire inconsistencies. I searched for classes and books and connected with a mentor to help with my growth in these areas. This allowed for the deprogramming of unhealthy coping mechanisms fostered during my childhood. I was able to approach difficult moments with sobriety, peace, and skill. I no longer needed to be impulsive in my responses because I embraced the pace of my life's journey. It brought on a peace that silenced any insecurity, inferiority, and comparison.

Gracefully, my homelessness journey of three years ended on a stable note. I'd established my consulting agency, Bloomin' Queens Co. We strive to empower women as they heal, grow, and lead under the safety of sisterhood. I've hosted different events that created a safe space for men and women to have candid conversations on intimate topics such as love and healthy interactions. I believe that every woman should bloom at her own pace! This business was incubated during one tumultuous personal journey, yet it has liberated many women to simply be.

Chapter 13

Earnestly, I've made a life commitment to empowering women through the acceptance and healing of their stories. My responsibility as a wellness consultant isn't taken lightly or hidden. I'm a lifelong learner determined to continue to bloom at my own pace. No amount of success, opportunity, or exposure will diminish the priority of my growth. In addition, my family has embraced the pace of their individual lives as well. And I'm esteemed to know that every woman reading my story will walk away empowered and convicted to analyze the quality of their wellness!

Bio

Nadia O. Hill is a graduate and current Alumni Board Member of the University of Illinois at Chicago (UIC). As a GED instructor, she served as an AmeriCorps member from 2012-2014. Currently, she works at Breakthrough Urban Ministries as the Associate Director of High School and Post- Secondary Programs. She has assisted over 100 survivors impacted by violence by securing supportive resources.

She is passionate about healthy living, personal development, and advocacy. Also, she hosts panel discussions, virtual events, and live teachings on topics such as mental health, holistic wellness, and identity. In addition, she has established her business, Bloomin' Queens Co., which strives to empower women as they heal, grow, and lead under the safety of sisterhood. She has partnered with over 1000 women blooming at their own pace. And she is dedicated to pushing the message that Godly femininity is a seat of authority!

Chapter 14

Abused but not Broken
By Devon Croom

Facing colorism during my elementary years wasn't fun. The kids in my neighborhood were rude. I was part of many jokes such as "Devon, you're black as tar" or "This tire is lighter than you." I recall my mother going to my school to confront a little boy who said my penny loafer shoes were ugly. This was followed by mental health challenges due to being surrounded and raised by family members who also suffered from mental health, alcoholism, and substance abuse. It turned out for the worst when I moved from Newport News, Virginia, to Naples, Italy. My self-esteem was low because I was always told how 'black and ugly' my skin was. I can't recall ever being told I was beautiful or loved. I desired the attention to be wanted, loved, and appreciated. Being in Italy, the Italians enjoyed the sight of a black woman. I recall one time a male got out of his car, stopped traffic then ushered my mother and me to walk across the street. Quickly things shifted for the worst.

At school, life was great. I was top of my class with grades and enjoyed my friends. However, at home, it was different. I experienced physical, verbal, and emotional abuse. My stepfather and I never got along because I repeatedly declined sexual advancement. I recall one night, I woke up

Chapter 14

to him kneeling next to my bed. My panty was off, no blanket or sheets were over me, and the room was dark. I recall his voice as if he had said it yesterday, "Be quiet and go back to sleep." My mind blanked out. In addition, we got into multiple fistfights; however, this last fight cost him his career in the United States Navy. I was sent back to Virginia to live with my grandparents. Although I was freed from the abuse there, the abuse continued to follow me.

Returning home to Newport News, Virginia, was exciting. I was back with my friends and family. However, the substance abuse and drug usage of my family members increased. Seeking love in all the wrong places, I became pregnant at the age of 15. Unknowing me, my mother took me to an abortion clinic. While at the table, the nurse asked me if I was ready. I asked, "Ready for what?" When she explained what my appointment was for, I quickly got dressed, declined service, and listened to my mother share with me during our commute home how much of a disgrace I was. I ran away from home and moved in with my child's father. I delivered my son at the age of 16. Just when I thought I would experience love, he started to beat me. I was hit if I disagreed with him, lost a game of spades, or did not follow his command. When you don't know what love is, what it feels like, or have never heard the words 'I Love You,' you will accept anything that comes your way. I did just that to avoid going back to the home I was raised in. I love my family; I am not a fan of their choices in life. So, I tried to create a happy home of my own.

I got married and had two more children, trying to beat the odds of having children by the same person. Statistics said the average young married couple would last no more than five years of marriage. For years, things were going great. My husband became ill, and our marriage began to decline. My children were old enough that they noticed the abuse, so I made the hard decision to leave the marriage. He told me, "Who will marry a black, ugly mother of three with no money?" Whelp, I heard that before. In addition, I never received counseling for my abuse as a child, and now, as a divorcee. I made up my mind; I had to make a change for my children's sake. By the way, many people who truly knew my story always asked why I hadn't written a book to tell my story. A book? It's not over until God says it's over.

Now I recognize the lack of therapy from my childhood negatively impacted my relationship with my mother, my parenting skills, and my dating. I healed by leveraging several resources. I had therapy. Increased my spiritual life with Christ and spoke with a few church leaders as my confidants. I relied on prayer warriors and a trusted circle of friends. I ensured my children participated in grief counseling when their father passed away due to illness. After I learned more about God, he taught me a lot about myself and my calling. I am pleased to say I got married to my soulmate. He makes me feel secure, loved, and cared for, unlike what I was told for many years. I know the feeling of abandonment, lack of support, and conditional love. I vow to be the change I want to see in the community and to be an inspiration to many who walked similar paths. I am excited to announce that I am a certified Life Coach and internationally known Author. My book, 'Abused But Not Broken' is available on Amazon. You can learn more about my story and services and purchase an autographed copy of my book by visiting www.devoncroom.com.

Chapter 14

Bio

Devon Croom is married to Darryl Croom, a retired, 20 years Navy Veteran. They have five children. Devon was born and raised in Newport News, Virginia. She and her family reside in Cumming, Georgia. Devon enjoys traveling, reading, and fellowship with friends and family.

Devon is a graduate of Regent University. She has a master's in organizational leadership and a minor in human resource management. She embraced her calling as a shepherd and integrated her passion for developing others in each role and the task she is assigned. Devon's servant leadership skills have been leveraged in several organizations' platforms such as Women in Cable Telecommunication (WICT), National Association for Multi-Ethnicity in Communications (NAMIC), Diversity, Equity & Inclusion (DE&I), National Black MBA Association (NBMBAA) and Black Employee Resource Group (BERG).

Devon published her memoir, 'Abused But Not Broken,' in June 2020. It's available on Amazon. She is a certified Life and Marriage Coach. She's the founder of DC Consulting 7LLC firm. Devon is a woman with experience, passion, and servant leadership who inspires, motivates, and empowers everyone she meets.

Devon integrates work and life with the guidance of God (spirit of discernment). She doesn't look at her assignments from God as work; it's her calling and passion. Devon quotes, "God must be first in everything you do. I pray my trials and tribulations become your inspiration and motivation."

Chapter 15

Intimacy has a Sound
By Jessica Shepard

I grew up going to church, but I also grew up in trauma. My parents got divorced when I was 5, and I lived with my mom. When I was about 10, my mom left, and I moved into my dad's house. And when I was 13, I had to move in with my grandma. I am the oldest of three. My sister ended up moving to GA with family while my brother and I lived with our paternal grandma. I never understood why we were separated. Growing up, my sister and I were extremely close, but once we were separated, we grew apart and didn't become close again until we were in our twenties. My stepmom burned our house down when I was in 7th grade, and we lost everything. I remember the S.W.A.T. team coming to my house when I was in elementary school because of something the man my mom was dating did. And my dad was always in and out of the picture because he was a drug addict which was hard. After all, I was always a daddy's girl.

From the age of 10 until about 25, I struggled with rejection heavily. I can vividly remember nights sobbing, thinking that if my parents didn't want me, why would anyone else? I can also remember nights feeling angry at God for letting me go through the things I went through, then

Chapter 15

feeling guilty for being angry. All those experiences began shaping my view on relationships. Before we experience a relationship with God, we experience relationships with family or the people that raise us. Those relationships set the tone for how we respond to the people around us, and for me, it set the tone for how I responded to God.

I mentioned that I grew up in church but growing up in church and having a relationship with God are completely different things. I grew up in a holiness or hell household. Doing the right thing wasn't out of love for God but out of fear of going to hell. I always felt like I had to try to be good enough for God. And when I wasn't, I felt like I wasn't good enough even to approach him in prayer. I lived my life in guilt and shame. After high school, I stopped attending church and thought I was living my best life. I was partying, getting drunk, and doing things I was not proud of. But it got old. I started to grow up, and I realized how unhappy I was. Then someone told me about the Disney College Program. I live in VA, and I also love everything Disney does. I applied, got accepted, and didn't look back. I was so happy to move to FL.

Once I was there, I started to struggle because I had no friends or anything that could distract me. All my issues started screaming at me to deal with them, and I didn't know what to do. Then while grocery shopping, looking for chips, a lady stopped and asked me if I had a church home. I told her no, and she handed me a flyer. The day before, I told myself I wanted to try and find a church after being out of church for almost 7 years. I took that as a sign, and I went. I ended up connecting with a woman at that church who helped me get back on track. That was in 2013, and nine years later, we are still friends.

I ended up moving back to VA in 2014 and tried different churches until I found one that I loved in 2018 and joined a month after my first visit. I grew in ways I didn't even know were possible. But in 2020, everything shut down because of the pandemic, and I was left in a similar situation as when I moved to FL. I was isolated with nothing to distract me from my issues, but this time they were issues I didn't even know I had. I was trying to please God by serving and thought he was happy with me. But I had nowhere to serve with the church being closed, and I realized my relationship with God was based on serving and not on spending time with Him. It was then that I realized I had no idea how to have relationships with people. My trauma response to people please became my everyday life. My church has the most amazing women. They genuinely love and care about me, but I always kept them at a distance because of the trauma I experienced growing up. And I always kept God at a distance because I allowed my relationship with nature to influence my relationship with Him. I was comfortable doing things for people and God as long as I didn't have to get too close personally.

I have learned that before we can open up to the people around us, we must open up to God first. Numbers 23:19 says, "God is not a man, so he does not lie. He is not human, so he does not change his mind. Has he ever spoken and failed to act? Has he ever promised and not carried it through?" He is not intimidated by our hurt, disappointment, doubt, or anger. Our feelings do not and will never change how he feels about us. Intimacy has a sound, so I challenge you to speak out loud to God, no matter how awkward it feels. Tell him exactly what is on your heart and see how your relationship with him, and the people around you begin to grow. I would be lying if I said this is a change that can happen overnight. I am still working on opening, but I have started to believe that the women I am connected to do love me because I am finally beginning to believe that God genuinely loves me.

Bio

Jessica Shepard is an author and educator currently living in Virginia Beach. Shortly after publishing her first book "Bible Alphabet Book, Big Ideas for Little Minds," she was nominated for a nonfiction author award and a children's book award by Black Authors Rock. Jessica's creativity began as a child doing arts and crafts, then flowed into music. She developed her leadership skills while marching for Norfolk State University's Spartan Legion Marching band. Using her leadership skills and love for children, she became the team lead of the youth ministry at her church. Jessica has written curriculums and training for multiple churches since she began working with children. Her passion is to see youth develop a relationship with God in a fun, creative, and relevant way.

Chapter 16

Delivered and Set Free to be Me, God Did It!

By Antoinette Hines

As I navigated leaving a narcissistic relationship, I was in a season of darkness and confusion. This type of relationship will confuse you about what you believe, who you are, your characteristics, and your emotions. You are alienated from everyone you are in relationships with outside the narcissist. Every word is turned against you, and all conversations are centered on that person. There was constant humiliation and degrading of my thoughts. Experiencing a lot of gaslighting and love bombing had me on a rollercoaster ride of emotions. I lost myself, my sense of right and wrong, my voice, and my belief in what was inside me. The flame to serve was lost, and the desire to be among people in ministry diminished because he was a Minister in church. My confidence in what God placed inside me and my passion for teaching the word of God was suffocated. The narcissist, Dr. Jekyll and Mr. Hyde look good in the eyes of the public and ministry, but behind closed doors, it was torcher. Literally in tears in my closet, I cried out to God to be released from that relationship and be made whole again.

Chapter 16

Having my joy restored, peace back, and ability to be obedient to God was a priority. I missed being around people who truly loved me. There was a need to be ignited again in my passion. God honored my prayer.

Therapy was necessary to uproot the trauma and break the suppression and depression. God was exposing the spirits I had encountered through the relationship. The Absalom Spirit, Python Spirit, Orphan Spirit, Leviathan Spirit, and Spirit of Oppression; it was a long walk-through deliverance and the beginning of recovery. I recognized I was looking at a man's potential that never met the present man. Taking responsibility and accountability for my part in the relationship and all that I gave away was important. Releasing my heart, power, passion, and inner voice and not listening to my spirit opened the door. I freely yielded to the demands and requests of that person. I acknowledge the manipulation was because of an unmet need inside of me that I should have taken to the Lord. It was the beginning of finding myself again and the continual removal of the residue. Praying and seeking God was the greatest part of me walking back into being self-aware and checking the mirror of my own life.

I had to reintegrate with friends and family, learn to trust people and leaders in ministry, and lastly, find the confidence in my voice again. In October 2020, I saw a flyer on my classmate's story about a "Killer Confidence" conference by Destiny Inspire. A prayer was answered immediately, and I registered right away. During the conference, I heard powerful women talk about excelling in mental health, breaking barriers in business, overcoming obstacles, and walking in confidence. Closing out the Killer Confidence Conference, Destiny gave her testimony which hit my spirit and let me know it was time to take my voice back and rebuild my confidence. So, I signed up for Sis' Speak Up in November 2020, the first of her series. Destiny allowed space for us as women to release pain and walk into power. She cultivated our voices to tell our individual stories and move into prayer. Destiny opened a space of encouragement, celebration, and empowerment, where each woman evolved without competition or comparison. She stirred my passion for teaching the word of God again by allowing me to lead morning prayer calls on her platform, which was an honor and privilege. Destiny was the reason I got my confidence back, trusting God in my process and continuing to walk out of my passion. Under the reconstruction of me, with Destiny's help, fear broke off, and doubt diminished. Because of the confidence I gained, I met the love of my life and trusted God in him to become my life partner. Destiny, we both thank you!

Acknowledgments:

Chavon Annette, The Fire Leadership Coach, walked the word and fanned the flames that were ignited within me. She walked the text and had me check the mirror to see where I was and where God desired to take me. No more hiding; it was time to emerge and use my voice. Someone is waiting to hear the sound being released by God through me. Chavon lives by this saying without apology, and I love it.

Dr. Sonya Hawthorne, a Pastor, fire-baptized, Holy Spirit-filled, mighty woman of God, saw me when I was trying to readjust from ministry hurt. Frustration and doubt had come upon us about ministry. My husband and I have encountered so many wolves that scatter the sheep of God all too often, which led us to not want anything to do with ministry. But God has a way of restoring and reviving our love for ministry and people. Dr. Sonya ignited me to seek the Lord even more and trust what he placed within me. God, through Dr. Sonya, taught us to pray for those who spitefully used us and slandered our name. She saw our hearts and spoke to our Spirits to continue working unto the Lord and let God handle the rest. She holds me accountable and weighs my words as she continues to develop, train, and mentor me into my destiny. Thank you for your consistency and love for God!

Finally, my covenant sister, Communication Strategist, Elder Marcia P. Brown. She is an answered prayer to have a true sister near me that

Chapter 16

would hold me accountable and understand the process of where God is leading me on this journey. The river of God flows as hours seem like minutes, and the Prophetic bubbles over. Our hearts are so much alike for the things of God! I have the privilege of seeing God's hand moving in miraculous ways, propelling my faith and encouraging me to use my voice. Lord, here am I!

Bio

I am Mrs. Antoinette Hines, CEO of Uniquely Me, LLC., wife, mother of six beautiful diamonds, grandmother of two, and Minister. A two-time Amazon #1 Best-selling author, Amazon #1 International Best-selling author, speaker, mentor, Certified Fire Leadership Coach, Certified Christian Counselor Coach, Certified Leadership and Life Coach, blogger, and podcaster. Working with individuals to transform their mindset from Poverty to Prosperity by teaching and advising them on their finances is a passion. Impact, empower, impart, ignite, and position; I encourage everyone right where they are to save AND invest! I am a worshipper at heart, I love the Lord, and I am a faith walker in Christ. I look forward to walking on this transformation journey with people who want a better life. I am the MIRROR CHECK Queen!

Process your Pain and fulfill your Purpose with Power while Postured and Positioned through Passion, we gain Progress to be Productive!

Chapter 17

The Significance of a True Sister

By Lakeisha Lowe Yelverton

I distinctly remember many times when I needed a true sister to help me heal. Over the years, I've encountered severe hurts and pain inflicted upon me by the people I cared for the most. I had to learn how to forgive them and let go. I also learned to forgive myself for allowing those processes to hinder my forward progress in the kingdom of God.

I have sisters in Christ who poured into my brokenness, helping me move past some very dark times in my life. We never know what we will face in life, but I have concluded that all we go through is never for anything! There is purpose in it, and according to Romans 8:28, "And we know that all things work together for good to them that love God, to them who are the called according to his purpose." It works for our good! There comes that point in the life of a believer when our heart will be tested by what we say from our mouths.

Previously married for 17 years to a "Man of God," you would have thought life was grand! It started that way, but things changed, and I didn't understand why. Long story short, my ex-husband was habitually cheating on me with my twin sister. I'm thankful for this day that my

Chapter 17

sister found the courage to come forward and tell me the truth after years of questioning and seeking answers to my suspicions.

Believe it or not, part of my healing occurred with my twin sister going through the process with me. Because we have always been so close, it took both of us to walk through the healing process together to get past the hurt and move on with life. Some may find it strange that we got back to a place of love again, but God did that! We allowed Him to heal our hearts and minds. We were willing, and He was able to do it. A lot of talking and conversating went forth for months which turned into two years. But we got there through time. It took prayer, the word of God, and our faith to uphold us on that journey. In between that time, my best friend Marcy P. held me down! I cried on her shoulder many times. Every time I needed to talk, she was there. I joke about it now, but she was ready to "catch charges" on my behalf! I wouldn't have allowed her to do anything to cause that to happen, although my flesh was all in on the idea. Marcy helped me reason within myself and off the ledge of committing a crime that would alter my life. It wasn't worth it! Marcy gave sound advice, with lots of hugs and tears. She allowed me to bare my burdens on her shoulders.

My third sister, who helped me to heal, is Minster Michelle Williams. Now, this lady right here is special to me. One reason being she is the first cousin to my former spouse. One might assume that she'd take sides because of blood relations. She didn't. Instead, she remained close to me, being a friend indeed and sister despite any potential conflict of interest. Michelle sat with me for many days to let me vent! She never judged me, nor did she pity me. She was simply being a sister there for her sister in Christ in her hour of need. It was an unimaginable circumstance to be in. Betrayal on that level runs deep. Your emotions are everywhere, and the mind is bombarded with questions of why? It took lots of prayers and getting in the word of God to help me forgive and move past it all.

One of my mentors by the name of Apostle Catherine Newsome, I credit to this day for preaching a life-changing delivering word that spoke directly to where I was at that time. "Fight Sister Fight" was the titled message. I will NEVER forget that women's conference that night at Deeper Life Church Ministries! After the preached word, I found myself at the altar bent over in grief, hurt, and pain, sobbing like I never have before. Apostle Newsome prayed and laid hands upon me, calling out the deep hurt and pain inside. She decreed and spoke life and healing into my spirit that night. Immediately, I felt the release from the trauma attached to the situation. The pain was released as God did a work in me that night. It's only by God's grace I made it out of that process in my right mind. Broken and distraught are former descriptions of where I was. Now, I proclaim and walk in the fact that I am the healed of God!

The result of that event was a divorce. But, oh, how I praise God that it wasn't the end! Since then, I have been blessed to be found by my Boaz! Happily remarried my best friend for the past nine years. Life is good as we do it together. My husband knows me and supports all that God has called me to do. Our union afforded us a son together. Glory to God! I learned so much about myself and God during it all. He showed me another level of Grace, another level of who He is, and another aspect of my Purpose in this world. I thank God for it all, my sisters who were there by my side, and now the man of God who stands with me! Ministry was birthed out of this. Elevation has come, and I am living out the very thoughts and plans God the Father intended for my life from the beginning of time! For that, I give God praise. Today, I Pastor and own a business and non-profit, serving in the kingdom because I had sisters who helped me heal!

Bio

Pastor LaKeisha Lowe Yelverton is a woman of God who faithfully serves in the kingdom of our Lord Jesus Christ. A devoted wife to Ivory J. Yelverton, mother of four, and grandmother of two. She loves her family. LaKeisha accepted Christ at the age of 17. Serving in many capacities in the church, she grew in faith, and God saw her fit for elevation. She preached her initial sermon in November 2003, was ordained as an Elder in October 2006, then commissioned as Pastor of Destined for Purpose Apostolic Ministries.

Her journey allowed her to start a Non-Profit organization, "The Prayer Cell Ministry," serve as Assistant to Minister Charlotte Clark, founder of Sists2Sista Heart2Heart Women's Ministry, and become a first-time author of the book "Graced to Forgive," all while serving her local church under Apostle W.T. Ford. Pastor LaKeisha desires to see lives transformed through prayer and the power of God's word.

Chapter 18

Elevate Your Thinking
By Que Nona Guilford

God will use the experience to elevate your thinking about what he can do for you. As I tell my story, I challenge you to think about moments when you have limited God because of what is in your hands or your ability. You have dreams that God wants to turn into your reality. You have a vision that he will manifest through support and supply. Have an open mind so God can shift your perspective. You are closer than you think.

I was scrolling on social media and noticed that Pastor Sarah Roberts was having a conference in Dallas, Texas. I didn't have a job at the time because my health wasn't the best. I remember desiring to go but felt like I couldn't because I didn't have a job. Immediately, God revealed a vision of me worshiping at the conference, and I said to him, "God, if somebody pays for my plane ticket, I will trust you for the rest." I looked up how much a plane ticket, conference ticket, and hotel were because of Habakkuk 2:2. I went on with my day and paid some bills. I stopped relying on a job to pay my bills because God supplied my needs. When I pay people through certain apps, I like to call them to ensure they get it. I was on the phone with my PR, Laura Douglas, and she asked me

Chapter 18

how I was doing. I began to explain the vision that God showed me. I was so excited about it, as if it had already manifested on earth. She got excited and said, "Que Nona, I believe the Lord is telling me to pay for your plane ticket." WOW. I never told her about my promise to God. I immediately stepped out on faith and brought my plane ticket. I believed in God and what he was to do in my life.

The conference ticket was about to reach its closing date, and I got nervous. I started reminding God what he said. I didn't know how he would do it, but I knew he would. I had already connected to a few of Sarah Jakes Roberts's pages. I remember somebody had posted about extra tickets, so I inboxed her. She told me that she was selling a ticket for $40. Now, the regular ticket price was $199. This was a huge blessing. I began to share with her what God showed me and how He was moving in my life. I asked her again how much the ticket was just in case she changed her mind. She said, "Ma'am, just get there. Your ticket is paid for in full. I'm just going to sow this ticket into your life." WOW. Words can't describe the overwhelming feeling that I had in my heart. God was up to something, and it was bigger than me.

I am aware that my experience is not just for me. I have learned to ask God who is supposed to go with me because my atmosphere matters, and everybody around me add/subtracts to it. I asked a great friend if she wanted to go with me. After a few days, she decided to go on this journey with me. Looking back, I'm aware of why she was chosen. We were both nervous and unsure about what was about to happen, but we were willing to believe in God. We had some challenging moments that could have stopped us, but we were determined to win. God can't do anything new in your life if you are not open to change. When we limit God, we limit our experience with him. Yes, he can do it accidentally and abundantly in your life. Eph 3:20 He also gives us free will, so we have a choice to accept or not accept what he wants to do in our life.

As we drove to Atlanta to catch an early plane, we were so excited and expected God's move to overtake us. We didn't know much about

Atlanta airport, so we tried to stay focused on checking in. Once we got to Texas, our excitement grew like the Grinch's heart on "How the Grinch stole Christmas." We looked for an Uber to get to the hotel. When the driver told us it was $60, our anxiety kicked in that we weren't in small Dothan, Al. We must realize that God will stretch us before he elevates us. We were so unprepared, but God had us. When we got to the hotel and gave the person at the front desk our bags, we took a moment to refresh for the conference. Dora said, looking worried, "Que, I don't know if we made the right move because I wasn't expecting to pay $60 for a cab." I said, "God didn't bring us this far to leave us." Dora said with a laugh, "You act like somebody is just going walk up to us and give us some money or something." I said immediately, "I don't know what God is going to do but what we are not going to do is talk against what he might want to do. Let's go to this conference." She trusted God through me, so we moved with my faith.

When we got to the conference, they had already started, so we signed in and rushed to some seats on the first floor. Within 20 minutes of us getting in the building, we heard Pastor Sarah Jakes Roberts say, "Wait… I need to do this. I feel a heaviness in the atmosphere. Some of you'll just barely make it into the room. Like, barely made it, and God doesn't want y'all to go through the whole conference feeling like this. If this is you, please stand. Don't miss your blessing. If you have overflow, walk up to somebody standing and give them…$5, $10, or $20." I looked at Dora and immediately stood, then Dora stood up. Women came from everywhere to bless us. They sent $20 and $50. One woman sent $100. We had walked into the conference with a lack and walked out with overflow. We had enough to pay for our room and anything else we wanted. When God wants you to be in a room, he will provide. It is our job to believe; it is his job to perform.

Bio

Mrs. Que takes great pleasure in seeking after God's heart and desires to discover more of His will for her life through His word, so she began courses at Destiny Bible College in Dothan, Alabama. In February 2014, Que Nona launched her own business, Q's Touch, which specializes in candy tables and themes.

Mrs. Que is a domestic violence survivor, and with that being a significant aspect of her life, she desires to bring awareness to the issue in her community. A Change in Me Domestic Violence Awareness Event was birthed from her past experiences.

Mrs. Que authored five books: The Moments When God Touched, Gleaning to Legacy: The Next Generation, Gleaning To Legacy: The Next Level, Leaping Into Purpose, S.O.S. 30-day Devotional, Trusting God: My child to their Sailor, and Born 4 This. You can get more information on her website at www.mrsque.com. She also loves being a Mary Kay consultant.

Mrs. Que received the Inaugural Girlfriend Award in November 2018 and the Outstanding Community Service Award from Zeta Phi Beta Sorority in March 2019.

Chapter 19

Broken and Scorned
By Madelyn Jones

Who gets married to get divorced? No one I know of. But that's not how my story went.

February 2006, I married what I believed to be my lifetime love, but how swiftly things changed. Married yet alone, undergoing mental, emotional, and physical abuse. I kept it from my family and friends while trying to maintain my sanity.

I ended up pregnant six months into the marriage and was asked by my then-husband to have an abortion. I refused, and the abuse increased. My daily question was, "Why me?" I didn't understand what I had done to deserve this. I wasn't raised in this environment. "How did I get here?" I was wondering what I was being punished for. This can't be life. I battled depression and questioned my existence, all while being saved and knowing God.

I prayed and worshipped. Still attended church actively, hiding bruises. I masked my pain with a smile. I kept pushing because my unborn child deserved a chance. I was determined not to allow my seed - a promise of God - to die because of what I was enduring. My unborn child was my driving force during the worse season of my life.

Chapter 19

I felt like God wasn't speaking to me in that place. It was a hard and lonely time. I began to feel that my father had forsaken me. My family would reach out, and I would ignore the calls because I was shamed by the circumstances of my marriage and wanted no one to know. I isolated myself from everyone. It wasn't God-instructed isolation; it was all self-inflicted. That place of isolation caused me more harm than good.

For months, I pushed everyone away until I finally broke down one day. I called one of my closest friends and expressed what I had been going through. She didn't expose it, but she encouraged me. She would recite this passage of scripture, "And he said unto me, my grace is sufficient for thee: for my strength is made perfect in weakness. Most gladly therefore will I rather glory in my infirmities, that the power of Christ may rest upon me." 2 Corinthians 12:9

I would just listen and cry. I would talk to her daily up until my baby shower. The day of my shower was beautiful, and the love in the room was a sign of our Father's love for me. I felt safe, loved, valued, and appreciated. But truthfully, it was only for that allotted time. Truth is, I was broken, so my excitement was short-lived. I was broken and felt caged in by my current situation. But little did I know that help was soon to come.

A few weeks after my shower, I was ready to leave my then-husband, and it turned into a big fight. I called my good friend, and she said before we do anything, let us pray. She prayed, and I felt such peace come over me. She began encouraging me that the Lord was going to give me a strategy on how to exit this relationship, and it was sent on assignment to take me out. She began accompanying me to my final OB visits as prior, I went to them all alone. I felt myself regaining my strength and fighting to live again, not only for my unborn child but me. This relationship made me forget who I was, and the father sent this sister friend as angelic assistance to pull me out and hold me up. She would affirm me by the word of God and remind me of the power and authority I possessed.

I started responding to the chaos at home differently. I was no longer fearful nor phased by his attempts to agitate me. I began to connect more with my sister and a few other sisters who covered for me. Before home could get tensed, I pulled on my sister's community to gain strength and encouragement. My sisters were determined to see me win. After my son was born, I began to tell my sisters that during prayer, the Lord had shown me that by the time my son was eleven months old, I would be released from that situation. My sisters began to pray in agreement with me. I had days and cried many nights. However, I had finally stopped questioning God. I could hear him again and saw my EXODUS (exit). I was broken, hurt, and had endured a lot, but I saw the end of my tunnel. Joy was soon to come.

Eleven months to the date of the Lord speaking to me with my sisters and my mother holding my hands, I went and filed a restraining order as I was ready to get my life back.

Still broken, still hurting, but determined. I wanted the life God promised me and was willing to start over to attain it. Now, operating as a single mom, which was very challenging, my sisters supported me and allowed me moments to take a shower alone while they sat with my son. My sisters made me tend to my self-care and pushed me to reflect on my healthy habits before the marriage. My sisters urged me to get back in position with God. My sisters labored with me in prayer. They allowed me to cry as I grieved the failed marriage, offering me a safe place without judgment or rejection. My sisters never exposed my vulnerability to others. They guarded my heart at all costs.

My sisters helped me heal because they understood that my purpose would outlive and outweigh my brokenness. They sisters helped me heal by speaking the word of God over me. My sisters helped me heal by not only rendering words that they thought I wanted to hear but also by following through in action. My sisters helped me heal by helping me be restored to the place where I could have died. They would not let me be consumed by it because God allowed them to be my eyes to see beyond what I could see.

Sisterhood is vital when sanctioned by God! I am here because of some God-sent sisters who helped me heal and would not allow me to stay broken.

Chapter 19

Bio

Madelyn G. Jones is an affirmed Prophetess of the Lord's church. Prophetess Madelyn is an in-time voice. One commissioned by God to see His people healed, set free, and delivered. God has anointed and graced Prophetess Madelyn to walk and operate in the fivefold. The Apostolic anointing on her life builds and establishes those in leadership. She teaches God's people how to show up as their healed and whole selves, with love, power, and demonstration.

Prophetess Madelyn lives the consecrated life of an intercessor. The Wall Shatterers Ministry birthed this lifestyle. The place where walls built by life's circumstances are shattered daily, setting the captive free and destroying limits. As the ministry of Wall Shatterers continues to grow, God is launching the ministry of Prophetess Madelyn G. Jones.

Chapter 20

Incubator for Wholeness

By Sharnice Sherrod

As an only child in a single-parent home, I always wanted siblinghood. I've always been what most consider an "old soul" or "wise beyond my years," but that didn't negate the fact that I, too, wanted someone to look up to. Someone who lived a life before God, where I wouldn't have to question her reverence, faithfulness, or the curse word to many young girls, HOLINESS. My sister was always there (literally since before I could walk) because we grew up in the same church. But in 2012, something special happened. Our relationship started to sprout, and though there were others around, the way my sister walked in grace and dignity made her light shine far beyond the rest. And when my grandmother decided to let me go on my first trip without my blood family to AIM 2013, she said these words that I think changed both me and my sister's life:

"You can go, but you need to stay with Simone. She's the only sister I *trust* with you."

I was primarily raised by my grandparents, whom I love and respect dearly. Yet, their love did not negate my struggles with deep-rooted rejection, abandonment, insecurity, and rebellion, YOU NAME IT! I was

Chapter 20

MAD! MAD that my mother struggled her whole life. MAD that I couldn't have both of my parents. MAD that they just could not get along. MAD that I had to always choose between two opposing sides. MAD that my dad was married but my mother wasn't. JUST MAD!! Not to mention, I was this super spirit-filled church girl who dreamed heavily and saw spirits but lived a double life. So, you can imagine how I felt daily; lost, confused, empty, scared, and CRAZY, amongst other things.

Instead of using my anger for violence (well, at least not often), I used it to prove myself. To prove that I was good enough by going above and beyond in everything I did, from academics to friendships, to relationships, to church participation, I mean EVERYTHING! I grew up working double time to prove my value but was often left overused or dropped along the way.

My sister Simone changed that narrative for me. I never had to do anything to win her over or win her love or compassion. She was just… there! PRESENT! She gave without asking, counseled with no judgment, protected like a mother, and she loved with no conditions. In these next few moments, as you read, you will learn of pivotal moments in my history where *"my sister helped heal me."*

My adolescent years were filled with unhealthy friendships. I always tried fitting, leading me to act out of character, neglecting my true uniqueness. A common assumption about friendships is that people must be in the same age bracket and share similar experiences. Though Simone was 8 years older, we were able to build a genuine friendship. She taught me values and helped me overcome barriers so I could be authentic and unapologetic.

When I got the courage to walk away from an abusive relationship, Simone helped me pick up the pieces. I was promised the marriage, the kids, and the dream life that I didn't get to see or be a part of, but I was emotionally attacked and mentally manipulated every day for two years. She had recently moved to Dallas, Texas, so I tried to hide it, but when it all hit the fan, my sister's (and her very watchful husband's) protective antennas went ALL THE WAY UP! Every week, if not every day, they called me and talked me through the process. It was a long and gruesome process, and it took me almost another year to let go, but she was there in every single step. Even when we couldn't talk or I didn't have the words to say, her words lingered in my head and my heart. Simone's guidance and testimony led me on my journey to self-rediscovery and wholeness.

Simone's long-standing relationship with her husband, Anthony, also helped me heal. They showed and continue to show me that godly love is possible and not far within reach. From the day they met (on that same trip in 2013) to this day, I watched him love her with no limits. I watched my sister heal and progress into a woman of boldness and courage, and he never made her compromise her standards of holiness. That's why the testimony mentioned above was so powerful! And if she could do it, I know I can too.

This sisterhood was an incubator for healing and wholeness. It's been my safe space to learn and grow with grace. She led by example with class, virtuosity, strength, and beauty. Her prayers warred for me when I couldn't war for myself. I watched her on the floor in worship and prayer, and over time, she brought out the intercessor in me. Simone's wisdom has even guided me through progressively healing my relationship with my father. Now, he's one of my best friends. This sisterhood saved me and continues to be a space of love and development.

Today, I can say that her imprint on my life will be seen and felt by my daughters and mentees for generations to come. All because she chose me to be her baby sister and decided to be the big sister I needed.

To those reading this who feel broken, DON'T BELIEVE THE LIE; healing is possible for you too. My holiness and wholeness journey has been filled with pivotal failures and triumphs, and just like my sister helped heal me, I am committed to being the nurturing mentor, wise counsel, and sister for young women from broken homes like me. The story… is being written.

Bio

Sharnice Sherrod is a passionate administrator, mentor, strategist, and innovative entrepreneur from Suffolk, Virginia. She is an alumnus of the illustrious Norfolk State University, where she earned her Bachelor of Arts in Political Science with an emphasis in Public Administration and Paralegal Certification. She is currently pursuing her Master of Arts in Human Services Counseling at Regent University and plans to continue her education by obtaining a doctoral degree in Pastoral Counseling. Sharnice is the owner of BETHELIGHT COLLECTIVE, an online consulting agency that provides innovative life and business solutions so that entrepreneurs will effectively produce and progress in the marketplace. Sharnice is a nurturer at heart and uniquely combines coaching, consulting, and counseling principles to serve others with a transformative solution-focused experience. She believes that a person's business is as healthy as they are and provides regular accountability to her client's personal and professional whole wellness.

Chapter 21

Seven Hundred Miles Never Felt So Close

By Brittany Daisy

I left my family to follow my husband, a decision that I was fully prepared for and do not regret. But with all the readiness in the world, I wasn't prepared for the consecutive events of loss that I would soon experience. My husband was away for work more than he was home, and I was experiencing death, loss, and separation at a rate that felt like the speed of light. I was in a new place where everything I knew to be familiar with was in question. Marriage looked much different than I expected, friendships were changing, and I felt like a rose being forced to grow from concrete. The loss of my grandmother, father, and first child was devastating. I couldn't catch my breath. I was drowning, screaming for help... silently. Amid my most challenging season, God sent me an angel that would stick beside me through it all. I've always been the "friend" type of girl and blessed to have good friends, but this one was different. This was deep, this was intimate, it was honest, and it was edifying. Unlike most friendships, it wasn't birthed because of proximity. This friendship was birthed because of purpose and grew because of authenticity and vulnerability. This experience has been a true "My Sister Helped Me

Chapter 21

Heal" moment in my life. There are a few key components that aided in the healing process that I believe will allow every reader of this book to help another sister, friend, or spouse truly heal. My sister helped me heal through Authenticity, Vulnerability, Edification, and Balance.

Let's start with what I believe to be the most important, *Authenticity*. I don't know many people who would choose to have a fake friend, but unfortunately, sometimes we find ourselves in situations that lack integrity and authenticity. When building a God-ordained friendship/sisterhood, authenticity must be the foundation. It can be scary to show up as our true selves. We all have complex layers and cracks beneath the surface that we want to mask, and most times, we hide these things with no ill intent; this is how we protect ourselves. It's natural to want to show up as the best representative of yourself but often, showing up as your flawed self is the best way to honor and meet relational expectations. When authenticity is the foundation, healing can begin. Authenticity is freeing, liberating, and necessary. Authenticity creates a standard of respect and opens the door to healing. We all know that healing is not always pretty; it is a whirlwind of emotions and inconsistent. Healing, at times, can feel more like a punishment rather than a liberating experience. It can be heavy. What I found was a sister that helped me carry my load. During our very honest conversations, I found the freedom to expose my flaws and found safety in the reciprocated authenticity of my sister.

After the authenticity was established, the next stage of my healing came through *vulnerability*. Having a safe space to be vulnerable allowed me to show up as my authentic self and allowed me to explore things I was afraid to face. My sister challenged me to dig deeper. It's important to note that there's a huge difference between someone prying into your business versus genuinely probing to help you go beyond the surface. As we built our friendship and embarked on this healing journey together, vulnerability was essential. As we discussed different experiences and characteristics we embodied, we had to be vulnerable; it was terrifying but therapeutic and healing. My sister provided me with a space where I could pour my heart out. I released my innermost thoughts and greatest insecurities, and my sister collected them with love and care. There were many harsh truths and frequent tears but so many moments where we could feel God's presence through the phone. These moments of vulnerability were often unexpected, but it was like doors being unlocked and literal chains breaking off my heart. God promised that when two or three gather in his name, he would be in the midst. My healing process is a promise fulfilled.

What started as a new and unfamiliar place effortlessly became a safe space for me. We showed up as our true selves. We dug deep and challenged each other to heal old wounds. We would pray together and for each other. We shared our dreams and fears, and we held each other accountable. This is *edification*. Edification is defined as the instruction or improvement of a person morally or intellectually. From a biblical context, edification references the "building up and strengthening" of the church, and this is exactly what we experienced. I discovered and was challenged to truly walk in the calling God had destined for me. As I progress and reflect on the roughest moments of this journey, I think about the countless conversations that ended with me feeling full and a little more whole. Through our friendship, "church" was redefined for me, and I experienced God on a new level.

The last piece of the process is balanced. As I reflect on the many transitions that took place and the unpredictable grief that I experienced, I realize that although I was consumed with my storm, I was able to help her heal as well. It was so fulfilling to not only be poured into but also to refill my sister's cup. We discovered a beautiful balance between our give and take. We respected and challenged each other. We held each other accountable while extending grace. She held me down, lifted me, and gave me my flowers. As I enter a new stage of my life, I must give thanks and honor to the friend and sister that heard my silent tears. Thank you, my Diamond, for always being just a phone call away. And although 700 miles away, thank you for being receptive, present, and committed to my healing journey. I am a better woman, wife, follower of Christ, and friend because my sister helped me heal.

Bio

Brittany Daisy is a published Author, Stylist, and Doula. From her personal development journey, she discovered her purpose to help women become the best version of themselves from the inside out.

In 2012, Brittany Co-founded and led the Personal Development division of a women's organization. She has mentored over 30 young women focusing on education and self-discovery.

In 2020, Brittany created a virtual outlet for women to focus on mental health and self-care. She engaged women across the USA with weekly activities, live streams, and holistic beauty regimens.

In April 2020, Brittany Daisy published Letters To Freedom, a guided prayer journal. She has been featured on multiple podcast shows, invited as a motivational speaker for groups of women, and led virtual book club sessions. Brittany is committed to using her diverse experience and skill to guide her clients into a celebration of womanhood.

Chapter 22

Her Life Saved Mine
By Alexis Ganier

They tried their best to explain what was going on to me and my sisters, but nothing could ever prepare us for this kind of pain. They sat us down to tell us that the only person we knew loved us would not be around for a while. At the time, I had no real emotion toward what I heard. I didn't know how to process my feelings. I sat there quietly. I had no clue how this would impact my life in such an inordinate way. As a young teen, I heard what they were saying, but I just tucked away the information and kept going.

Losing your only consistent support in life is one of the hardest things ever. This was only temporary, but it happened at one of the most pivotal times in my life. I was a freshman in high school when my mother had to turn herself in. It was so much chatter going on around my sisters and me. We had no idea what would take place but all we knew was that we had each other. Once my mom was gone, I and my sisters were together, but as the years progressed, we were eventually separated. It was blow after blow, and all the suppressed sadness eventually came out and formed depression. I'm not sure if our family knew how much this affected us, but I do know they tried their best to support us. It still didn't take away the fact that all that we knew and were familiar with was taken away. We needed each other more now than ever. I heard a saying, "Sometimes you must **go** through to **get** through."

I believe this is especially true, just like the children of Israel. They had to go through the wilderness to get to the Promised Land. My life has been much like the children of Israel. There is a purpose in the wilderness. I've had to experience some hard times in the wilderness. In this process, I have learned so much that has made me a better me. I looked forward to the day my family would be back together.

As the years forged forward, we faced so many difficulties. It was hard on us as children, but we made it through. And when the final year came, by then, many things had changed. We weren't the young kids she had seen when she left. I had a three-month-old baby boy. Surprise, mom! (laughing) As she returned, she came back on a mission to get things in alignment. It's amazing how one event can alter the trajectory of your life. God had changed my mom's life, and there was a joy that we couldn't explain. There was a burning fire that no one could put out. She was different! The Lord told me to HONOR my mother!

I am dedicating this chapter to my mom, Diane Horn. I want to do that by giving special recognition and showing her great esteem. My mother deserves all accolades because she has shown my sisters and me what a real mother is.

*D*edicated: to loving each of us, especially her grandchildren

*I*nspiring: motivating us to finish well

*A*nswering every call

*N*urturing: always providing encouragement and support

*E*ffortlessly done the job of both parents

A woman like this isn't always born but built. My mom has faced many challenges in life and has overcome them. I know that there were things she wished that in her fight, we, as her children, didn't have to go through. But what the enemy intended to harm us, God intended it for good to accomplish what is now being done in each one of our lives. My mom has been everything a young woman could ask for, though there were years in between, and nothing has been lost. It's an honor to have a mother care about your soul. She prays for our family, and I know that her prayers have reached God's ears, and He answered. This chapter is called "Her Life Saved Mine" because it took some very hard things to happen in her life that ultimately changed my life. My mom is one of the reasons I am saved today. She stayed on me to live better than I had been, but she did it with so much love and grace. I am forever grateful to her because of how she handled the mission. God truly gets all the glory. Even to this day, my mom is dedicated to her children doing well in life and seeing the lives of other women flourish.

Mom, thank you for your heart for others. You have poured yourself into a measure that many would never understand. The love that exudes from you is contagious. You are dedicated to serving others and seeing them grow. You are a true leader that doesn't mind following. You have been a great model for women. Today, I hold your arms up. I'll forever pray for you. I love you with God's love and the depths of me. There is no me without you. God picked well when He made you my mom. I count it all joy for the things we had to go through. We are greater today because of it. You helped save my life. You helped me heal and grow. I know now that sometimes you must go down to go up. You have always been in the right place, and because of it, we have grown. You are a great example of a wife.

I love you and I will always honor you!

Chapter 22

Bio

Alexis Ganier was born in Oak Park, Il, where her resilient and relentless mother raised her. As a leader in the local church, what she was taught as a child has certainly paid off. Alexis' ability to lead with a heart of dedication and love has allowed her to reach many people. She actively leads the singles ministry, teaches, creates, heads the worship team, participates in mentorship programs, and works alongside her Pastors. Alexis enjoys building and developing others, so she desired to further her education to help the youth overcome many of their obstacles and difficulties. She attended National Louis University, where she got her degree in 2016, and she has a Bachelor of Arts in Applied Behavioral Science. When she's not busy assisting others, she enjoys spending time with family, relaxing, watching movies, writing, learning new things, and spending time with her son PJ.

Epilogue

An Unstoppable Force

Unstoppable- impossible to stop or prevent. We serve an unstoppable God who gives us the ability to be unstoppable. In this life, we face challenges, but we can rise above them all because of Him. This movement started with one yes in 2021, and all 2022, we have been knocking down walls and making the devil mad. I had no idea what it would evolve into, but if God had shown me the entire picture from the beginning, it would have seemed too hard to believe.

For an entire year, women have joined me in sharing their stories. They have made the courageous decision to come out of the shadows and share their stories with others so hope comes alive in another. This MOVEMENT has caused families to have serious conversations, giving people the opportunity to honor those that made an impact in their lives and even become a tool for professionals to use as a tool to help others. This movement has made it beyond the boundary lines of the United States, and I am so thankful and blessed for what God has done.

No matter what you have experienced in this life, you must understand that God has given you the power to rise above it and be victorious, thus

Epilogue

becoming an unstoppable force. When you choose to learn and trust in God, there are no limits to what He will do in and through your life.

Many people want to know more about my story as the visionary of this anthology. Well, in 2022, as all the anthologies were coming out, on the first anniversary of my leaving my job as a teacher, I share my story - the good, the bad, and the miraculous. That book is called FROM PAIN TO PURPOSE!!! Go order on my website or Amazon today. This journey has been women sharing their own stories!! This is not the end!! Stay tuned for 2023!!!

Visionary:

First and foremost, Chavon Anette is a daughter of God! She is the CEO of Purpose Unwrapped, LLC and non-profit Power and Grace Leaders, Inc. Chavon is affectionately known as the Fire Leadership Coach and is a Leadership Consultant.

As the Fire Leadership Coach, she marries practical and spiritual tools to empower and equip kingdom people to lead in the world.

She balances entrepreneurship, ministry, and employment as the Student Success Manager at Regent University. She enjoys creating experiences for holistic transformation, so she annually hosts two big events: Fanning the Flame Experience and Powerhouse Leaders Conference.

She is also a transformational speaker and minister of the gospel who speaks with great passion in a way that empowers and challenges her listeners. She has been featured as a speaker on ABC news, TCT Today, Atlanta Live, Norfolk State University, Virginia Wesleyan University, and at conferences and other events such as the globally recognized Comeback Champion Summit, Sister Leads Conference, and more.

Chavon has published 4 books that are available on Amazon, and she has been a part of 7 anthologies. From Pain to Purpose was her first solo project that became an Amazon #1 Bestselling book. She is the visionary of volumes of My Sister Helped Me Heal Anthology, which is an Amazon #1 Bestselling Anthology movement. Finally, Chavon Anette was the 2021 Servant Leader of the Year Award Recipient from ACHI Magazine.

www.ingramcontent.com/pod-product-compliance
Lightning Source LLC
Chambersburg PA
CBHW060033180426
43196CB00045B/2646